USY MANAGER'S GUIDE TO DELEGATION

THE BUSY MANAGER'S GUIDE TO DELEGATION

Richard A. Luecke
Perry McIntosh

AMACOM
AMERICAN MANAGEMENT ASSOCIATION
New York • Atlanta • Brussels • Chicago • Mexico City • San Francisco
Shanghai • Tokyo • Toronto • Washington, D.C.

*This publication is designed to provide accurate and authoritative
information in regard to the subject matter covered. It is sold with
the understanding that the publisher is not engaged in rendering
legal, accounting, or other professional service. If legal advice or
other expert assistance is required, the services of a competent professional person should be sought.*

Library of Congress Cataloging-in-Publication Data

Luecke, Richard.
   The busy manager's guide to delegation / Richard A. Luecke,
Perry McIntosh.
        p.   cm.
      Includes index.
      ISBN-13: 978-0-8144-1474-3 (pbk.)
      ISBN-10: 0-8144-1474-5 (pbk.)
      1. Delegation of authority.   2. Supervision of employees.
   I. McIntosh, Perry.   II. Title.

   HD50.L84   2009
   658.4'02—dc22

                                        2009009841

Printing number

10   9   8   7   6   5   4   3   2   1

CONTENTS

Preface   vii

Introduction   1

Chapter 1   Determine Which Tasks to Delegate   9

Chapter 2   Identify the Right Person for the Job   19

Chapter 3   Assign the Task   33

Chapter 4   Monitor Progress and Provide Feedback   49

Chapter 5   Evaluate Performance   59

Chapter 6   Typical Problems and How to Solve Them   73

Chapter 7   Five-Day Shape-Up Plan   87

Afterword   93

Glossary   95

Selected Readings   97

Index   99

PREFACE

One of the authors still recalls his first experience as a very low-level manager. It happened during the second week of army basic training. The platoon drill sergeant had made him his assistant—the platoon guide—and his first assignment seemed simple enough.

"Listen up," the sergeant barked. "There's some white paint down in the supply room. Get two cans of it up here on the double!"

The platoon guide ran down to the supply room, grabbed two buckets of paint, and raced back to the sergeant's small office, taking two stairs at a time. "Two cans of white paint, Sergeant!"

The drill sergeant assumed an expression of mocking bemusement. "Private," he began calmly, "you disappoint me. I said get that paint up here on the double, didn't I?"

"Yes, Sergeant."

"But I didn't tell *you* to get it." His face reddened as he shouted, "You were supposed to get one of those other maggots to fetch the damn paint!"

As you can see, this author's first test as a delegator ended ignominiously in failure. Fortunately, he survived that experience and learned an important lesson. What has been your experience as a manager or supervisor? Have you learned how and when and to whom to delegate, or are you still doing many chores yourself?

If you haven't yet mastered the art of delegation, this book will provide you with ideas and tips that you can apply today. Thankfully, the subject isn't one that's supported by mountains of research, so you won't encounter lots of boring academic studies and jargon. What you will find is a solid method and practical advice supported by both common sense and experience. Follow that method and you will be more effective as a manager or supervisor. You'll discover time you never had before—time for planning, budgeting, and motivating people.

So read on.

INTRODUCTION

Bob looks at his watch. It is almost 6 P.M. The last member of his sales support department has turned off her PC and headed out the door, leaving him alone in his cube with a pile of unfinished work and a visceral sense that he is ineffective in his work. Glancing at his calendar, Bob sees that the next day is packed with meetings and "to-do" items. With so much of today's business unfinished, he wonders what sort of dent he'll be able to make in tomorrow's workload. "It's true what they say about a manager's work," he tells himself. "There is too much to do and too little time to do it."

Bob's assessment is painfully true. There is seldom enough time to do everything that managers—and many supervisors—are asked to handle. Their days are punctuated by meetings, phone calls, business lunches, and emergencies that whipsaw their attention from one matter to another, leaving them little time in which to concentrate on the classic functions of management, which are to:

➤ Develop plans that will help the organization achieve its goals.

➤ Organize people and resources in support of plans.

➤ Direct and motivate people to work toward organizational goals.

➤ Control activities through budgeting, performance metrics, and other methods.

Attention to each of these important functions is often impossible in the crush of day-to-day work.

One of the important antidotes to the manager's chaotic situation is delegation. *Delegation* is a process through which managers and supervisors assign formal authority, responsibility, and accountability for work activities to subordinates. Fix those three terms in your mind: *authority, responsibility, accountability*. This process transfers those three qualities from one organizational level to a lower one. Delegation is rooted in the essential purpose of management, which is to *produce results through people*. Every level of management, from the CEO down to the frontline supervisor, must delegate in order to accomplish his or her goals.

. . . .

SIGNS THAT YOU'RE DELEGATING TOO LITTLE OR TOO MUCH

Are you up to your neck in work while your subordinates appear bored and have time on their hands? Do you find yourself doing many if not most of the same things you did before you became a manager or supervisor? Are other managers in your peer group less busy than you? Have you been unable to take a vacation because of the workload? Do your subordinates come to you for every decision?

If you answered yes to any of these questions, there's a good chance that you are delegating too little. Conversely, if you've delegated tasks that are parts of your core job description, or if you have time on your hands while your subordinates are burning out, then you may be guilty of overdelegation.

. . . .

WHY DELEGATING IS IMPORTANT

Delegating is important for a number of reasons:

- ➤ **Delegation addresses every manager's problem: too much to do . . . too little time.** If you are very good at your job, people will want even more from you—more than you can possibly deliver without help. If you delegate some chores, you'll have more time to plan, to organize, and to motivate.

- ➤ **Delegation fulfills every manager's responsibility to develop the workplace competencies of his or her subordinates.** By meaningfully involving other people in new tasks and challenges, you can develop their workplace skills. Employees often ask for training programs, but real assignments are usually the best career builders. If you delegate often and well, you will build a strong and successful team.

- ➤ **Delegation reveals the capabilities and shortcomings of subordinates.** You'll never really know what your people are capable of if you don't direct challenging new assignments their way. Consider the case of Joan, a friend of the authors. Joan was a literature major in college and began her business career as a secretary. Before long she was promoted to an administrative assistant position, working for the CEO. "Over a period of several years, the CEO delegated many difficult assignments to me," she recalls. "He liked to joke that he would give me harder and harder assignments until such time that I really screwed up." But she didn't screw up, so the CEO appointed Joan as the head of a newly founded subsidiary.

WHY SOME PEOPLE HOLD BACK

Some managers hesitate to delegate, often for the wrong reasons:

- ➤ **I can't trust anybody to handle this. I'll look bad if the job isn't done right.** Yes, there are things for which your subordinates are unprepared by training or experience. But for every one of those there are probably a dozen things you can entrust to them—especially if you have given them proper instruction and hands-on experience.

> **I can do this better than any of my people.** This is probably true, but this is no justification for you doing jobs more suited to other, lower-paid people. If you could file correspondence better than your secretary, should you make that part of your job?

> **I don't have time to explain how to do this job. It's faster and easier to do it myself.** Delegation requires up-front time and effort, making it seem faster and easier to do a job yourself. But there's an opportunity cost here: Time spent on tasks you could delegate is time that's not available for the higher-value activities that none of your subordinates are capable of doing. Also, as a supervisor or manager, you should be coaching your subordinates on how to do things. One of your jobs is to build their competencies—their human capital. If you're not doing that, you're failing in one dimension of your responsibilities.

> **I'm a doer!** New managers are just a step away from their previous roles as individual contributors. As individual contributors they developed technical mastery of certain tasks, and they received lots of recognition for that mastery. Many were promoted to management *because* of their success as individual contributors. Unfortunately, many new managers have trouble making the transition to their new roles. They remain happiest and most satisfied doing what they did so successfully in the past, and they are reluctant to let go. To enjoy success as a manager, however, you must learn to let go and turn your attention to the work for which you are uniquely responsible: making key decisions, planning, leading, motivating, and coordinating the work of others. If you fail to give these key responsibilities their due, you will fail to perform effectively.

> **I'm responsible for what happens here. I cannot delegate that responsibility.** I must stay in control. Some managers fail to delegate for fear that they will lose control. This is not a valid excuse. True, you hand over a measure of discretion and authority when you delegate a job, but you remain responsible to the organization for

the eventual outcome, no matter who does the work. You do not ab-dicate responsibility when you delegate work to others. The person who takes on the job, however, is responsible to you for its quality and timeliness. Thus, you retain control by virtue of the performance stan-dards you impose on your subordinates. As long as those standards are clearly communicated along with the task—and enforced—you will not lose control. The often unspoken subtext for this excuse for not delegating is managers' urge to control and micromanage. They fear that in delegating they will give away part of their authority (i.e., their power). Sharing authority, however, is essential in today's flatter organ-izations in which managers generally have many more direct reports. The fear of giving up control is alleviated when managers and their subordinates share the same sense of quality and accountability for results, and when they are aligned with a common set of overarching goals.

Are any of these excuses holding you back? If so, it's time to change—to begin looking for more opportunities to delegate work to people who can handle it.

- -

WARNING: FAILURE TO DEVELOP SUBORDINATES MAY COST YOU A PROMOTION

Some managers like to feel that they are irreplaceable. They feel se-cure in knowing that none of their people have the qualifications to challenge them for their jobs. "So why," they ask, "should we del-egate assignments that will teach our employees everything we know?"

That attitude won't get you far in an organization that puts a premium on employee development. And there's a practical down-side that many overlook: Managers with no immediate successors are often *stuck* in their jobs. The Big Boss says, "I'd like to promote Smith to a higher level, but his department couldn't possibly func-tion without him. It would take us a year or more to train or recruit a replacement."

So, don't feel threatened by your brightest subordinate. Instead, use delegation as a tool to groom that person as your successor. Doing so may free you up for a promotion!

. . . .

FIVE STEPS TO SUCCESSFUL DELEGATION

Once you've resolved to take advantage of the benefit of delegating, you need a method for doing it well. We recommend the five-step process shown in Figure I-1. The steps are simple and commonsensical—not rocket science. In the chapters that follow, we explain and offer practical tips for each step. Once you understand these steps, practice will give you mastery.

FIGURE I-1. THE FIVE-STEP DELEGATION PROCESS.

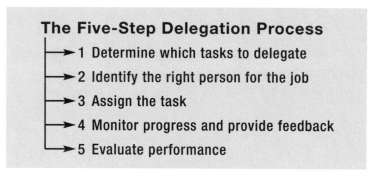

The Five-Step Delegation Process
1 Determine which tasks to delegate
2 Identify the right person for the job
3 Assign the task
4 Monitor progress and provide feedback
5 Evaluate performance

CHAPTER REVIEW

Try the following open-book review quiz to find out how much you've learned in this introduction:

1. How would you define delegation?

_____

_____

_____

_____

_____

2. Describe one sign that a manager is delegating too little.

_____

_____

_____

_____

_____

3. This chapter gave several reasons why delegating is important. Describe one.

_____

_____

_____

_____

_____

4. A new manager who doesn't delegate work may be showing that he or she hasn't effectively made the transition from individual contributor to manager. Why is this a problem?

_____

_____

_____

_____

_____

CHAPTER 1

DETERMINE WHICH TASKS TO DELEGATE

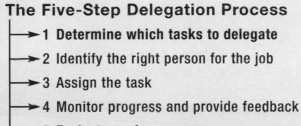

The Five-Step Delegation Process

1 **Determine which tasks to delegate**

2 Identify the right person for the job

3 Assign the task

4 Monitor progress and provide feedback

5 Evaluate performance

Helen has just received a phone call from her boss requesting that she take responsibility for the company's three-day orientation program for newly hired salespeople. The program includes some product training but is largely focused on introducing the newcomers to the departments and people with whom they will interact both in the office and while working in their assigned territories. "I like to pass this job around to our most successful sales managers," the boss told her. "I know that I can rely on you to do a great job."

The gratification she felt on hearing her boss's flattering words quickly fades as she stares into the screen of her work-scheduling software. Every day is crammed with deadlines, meetings, travel, customer appointments, and other obligations. Where will she find the five days she needs to plan and execute the orientation session? She can't say no to her boss's request, but she can't invent more hours and days either.

The solution, as Helen sees it, is to postpone some appointments and travel and to delegate some of her calendar and "to-do" items to other members of the sales team. But which items?

Helen faces one of the perennial decisions faced by all managers and many supervisors: In making the most of their limited time, they must periodically off-load certain work to others. But which should they retain for themselves and which should be delegated? To find the answer, let's jump right in with Step 1, which requires looking at all the things that weigh on your time and determining which can—and which cannot—be outsourced to others.

In principle, you should delegate as much as possible; doing so will develop the capabilities of your staff and give you more time for important and strategic work. You can delegate anything from simple tasks to decisions to entire projects or processes. Generally, you should consider delegating anything that your subordinates—considering their skills and available time—are capable of handling or can be trained to handle. These tasks will be determined by your situation. As you think about what you should delegate, be guided first by this question: What tasks are you now doing that do *not* require your unique knowledge, skills, or authority? The answer will identify *opportunities* for possible delegation. There's still no assurance that the right people with the right skills and sufficient time will be available to take them on.

SHARED AND UNIQUE SKILLS

You and your subordinates very likely share some skills in common (see Figure 1-1). These may be the ability to contact customers via telephone, by e-mail, or face-to-face; to generate monthly department progress reports; to schedule meetings; to keep track of when people plan to take their vacations; to check the accuracy of expense reports; to provide coaching to new employees; and so forth. The list of shared skills may be long, especially if you've worked your way up the ladder in the department. You had to learn all those things to get where you are now. And even though you're the manager, it's likely that some people have specialized skills you don't have. For example, the manager of an ad department may have no idea how to do what his graphic designer can accomplish. But there is also a skill set that is uniquely yours, things that only you can do by virtue of your training, experience, or authority. Budgeting, planning, sales forecasting, customer/supplier negotiating, effective meeting management, and mentoring are just a few of the skills that we normally think of as uniquely managerial skills. True, a sharp protégé may have mastered some of these skills, but few subordinates of lower or middle managers will have them.

Now that you understand the shared skill set in your work group, consider the many tasks you are personally handling that fall within that shared skill set. Remember, these are tasks you are doing that do *not* require your unique capabilities as a manager—things that *other* people could do. These may include developing monthly reports, set-

FIGURE 1-1. EMPLOYEE AND MANAGER SKILL SETS.

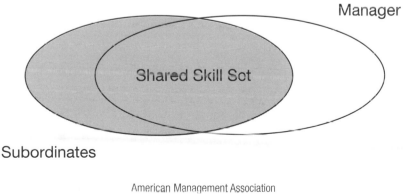

Manager

Shared Skill Set

Subordinates

ting up outside appointments, filing, or correspondence. To be systematic, make a list of these tasks, like the one shown in Figure 1-2. Now take a look at your list and ask yourself, "Which of these tasks could I reasonably delegate to someone else?" Put a check mark next to these. Don't worry about who will pick up these tasks. We'll get to that in the next chapter.

Whenever possible, identify *entire* tasks, not bits and pieces of jobs. By making one person responsible for an entire task, not only do you give that person a greater sense of control and responsibility, but you also avoid the coordination problems and "hand-off errors" that typically plague jobs that are delegated among several people. If the task is too large for one person to take it on, consider delegating it to a team. Delegating to a team is different from delegating different parts of a task to different individuals. A team can organize the work assigned to it and hold itself accountable as a group for the work's successful completion.

FIGURE 1-2. YOUR TASKS IN THE SHARED SKILLS SET.

Task	
Organize weekly meeting; reserve conference room.	✓
Coach Bill and Martha on the presentation to their big client.	✓
Update monthly sales figures.	✓
Download e-mails.	✓
Participate in weekly staff meeting.	✓
Send sales material to the field sales staff.	✓
Distribute customer comments to field and office personnel.	✓

DELEGATE RECURRING TASKS

When you're considering tasks to delegate, an easy way to begin is to list tasks that recur frequently or regularly. Recurring tasks, such as the following, show up at all levels of the organization and require different levels of skill:

➤   Reserving a conference room and ordering lunch for the weekly sales meeting

➤   Reviewing inventory levels and placing regular orders

➤   Checking the accuracy of expense reports submitted by your people

➤   Updating the monthly budget report with the latest sales and expense figures

Almost by definition, these tasks become routine, which means that once you've shown someone how to handle them, you won't have to show them again. By contrast, a onetime chore may not be worth delegating, given the time you'll have to invest in training someone to do it right. The time available for training and overseeing progress should always become part of your calculus in deciding what to delegate. True "onetime chores," however, are rare in the business world.

THE QUALITY ISSUE

Quality is the final issue to consider in identifying tasks to delegate. By *quality* we mean a job done right and on time. This issue must be foremost in your mind whenever you delegate. Ask yourself the following questions:

➤   Is the task so technical that extensive coaching will be necessary to bring the delegatee to a high level of proficiency? Your schedule

may be too overloaded to take on a big coaching project at this
time (but do incorporate it into your future plans so you can move
this task off your plate).

➤ Is there enough time to recruit the person and explain how to
do the job? If a deadline is just around the corner, you may not
have time to accomplish this.

➤ What's "good enough" for this task? Will an "adequate" job be satisfactory, given the nature of the task? Not every task requires a
master's touch.

➤ What will be the consequences of a job done poorly? If the consequences of less than perfect performance are manageable, then
you can start an employee on the learning curve and monitor the
outcome. If perfect execution is critical to the achievement of a
major goal, consider the risk you'll be taking in handing it off to a
subordinate.

TASKS THAT *NEVER* SHOULD BE DELEGATED

A few essential managerial activities should stay with you and *never* be
delegated to others. These include hiring, performance review, firing
and disciplinary actions, and certain specific tasks that have been delegated to you by someone else.

Hiring

It's usually a good idea to seek your subordinates' insights about job
candidates. Many managers routinely ask their people to meet with vis-
iting candidates to describe workplace routines and answer any questions the candidates may have. Afterward, they share with managers
their impressions of the candidates. This collaboration benefits everyone. It is important that candidates understand the environment of the
job for which they are applying, and it is equally important that current
employees get a chance to interact with these individuals who may be
joining their work group as peers. Southwest Airlines, the most successful company in its industry, uses a panel of employees from different

levels and functions to interview and screen job applicants. The final decision, however, remains with the manager for whom an applicant will work. Subordinate input to the decision is fine, but hiring is not something that can or should be delegated.

Along this same vein, you should retain the job of selecting people for project teams. Be open to advice, but make these selections yourself.

Performance Review

Many companies use annual *performance review* sessions to appraise employee performance, identify areas in which the person needs training or coaching, and communicate employee goals for the coming year. Is this one of your company's routines? These reviews, based on face-to-face meetings between managers and their direct reports, are also used to make decisions about bonuses and promotions. Naturally, performance review is a responsibility that stays with you; it cannot be delegated. However, you should be aware that there is a mechanism through which employees can legitimately weigh in on the workplace performance of others—including their own bosses. It's called *360-degree feedback*. With this appraisal method, anonymous information about an individual's workplace performance is collected from people who regularly interact with that person: subordinates, work team members, and "internal customers." In most cases, 360-degree feedback provides an assessment of an individual's performance that is more balanced and informed than the traditional boss's assessment of a subordinate. If your company uses "360s" you may have access to some overview material from these reviews (the details are usually confidential for the person being reviewed). Still, the formal appraisal of an employee's performance measured against his or her objectives is a task that stays with the manager.

Firing and Disciplinary Actions

Just as a manager cannot delegate a hiring decision, he or she cannot delegate actions that involve dismissing or disciplining anoth[er] [em]ployee. That responsibility remains with the manager, even managers almost universally point to firing and disciplinary actions as their *least* favorite responsibilities. That responsibility is tempered in some workplaces—especially in team-oriented workplaces—by peer pressure on slackers. High-performance work teams, especially those paid on the basis of measurable output, are intolerant of members who will not or cannot carry their own weight. For example, work teams at Nucor Corporation, a highly productive and profitable steelmaker, have a reputation for being very self-directed and self-disciplining. Because inefficiency by one person hits all team members in their pocket-books, slothful members are pressured by their peers to either clean up their act or look for work elsewhere.

Certain Tasks That Have Been Delegated to You by Someone Else

Let's suppose that your boss has delegated a job to you: She wants you to make an analysis of all suppliers used by your division, noting the level of business each does with all departments and examining the record for possible conflicts of interest. Normally, you could sub-delegate the task of compiling a list of suppliers and their sales to one of your subordinates, assuming that you have someone capable of do-ing the job correctly. However, this may be a situation in which your boss (or someone else) has delegated the job to you with the under-standing that *you alone* will handle it. Perhaps the job requires a level of trust or confidentiality that the boss sees you as uniquely qualified to handle. Perhaps it's a sensitive matter, or, for political rea-sons, the boss wants someone with managerial status to be seen do-ing the job. Whatever the reason, you must be alert to situations of this type and recognize that you must handle it yourself. If you are not sure, ask your boss.

. . . .

TAKE A BALANCED APPROACH TO THE DIRTY WORK

If your workplace is like most others, there are lots of different tasks to be done. Some will be interesting, motivating, and educational; others will fall in the "dirty work" category—the type that no one wants to do, because they are either boring, physically taxing, or otherwise unpleasant (e.g., dealing with a dissatisfied customer). As you consider the tasks you'd like to delegate, save a few of these unlikeable ones for yourself. You'll earn more respect as a leader if people see that you are willing to share in the hardships and not keep all the most pleasant and appealing jobs for yourself. Also, spread the dirty work around; don't give all the desirable jobs to one set of people and all the unpleasant or undesirable ones to another set.

. . . .

CHAPTER REVIEW

Try the following open-book review quiz to find out how much you've learned in this chapter:

1. What is the first question you should ask to identify tasks you might delegate to others?

_____

_____

_____

_____

2. A "shared skill set" is a set of skills that you and your subordinates share. What skills do you and your subordinates have in common?

_____

_____

_____

_____

3. Why is it a good idea to delegate entire jobs, not parts of them?

_____

_____

_____

_____

_____

4. List at least three tasks that a manager should never delegate to a subordinate.

_____

_____

_____

_____

_____

5. How should you handle delegation of unpleasant tasks?

_____

_____

_____

_____

_____

CHAPTER 2

IDENTIFY THE RIGHT PERSON FOR THE JOB

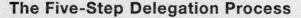

The Five-Step Delegation Process

1. Determine which tasks to delegate
2. **Identify the right person for the job**
3. Assign the task
4. Monitor progress and provide feedback
5. Evaluate performance

Helen, whose situation we encountered at the beginning of the previous chapter, needs to clear five days of previous commitments from her calendar in order to comply with her boss's request that she run the orientation program for new salespeople. She immediately reschedules three travel days, leaving just two days of other commitments to clear away. "There's no way that I can cancel, reschedule, or delegate a day's worth of that work," she tells herself, "but I can enlist some help with the job of preparing for the orientation program."

With that strategy in mind, she makes a short list of prep work that has to be taken care of prior to the event (see Figure 2-1). She quickly sees that she will have to do two tasks herself, and share another task with someone else—someone with experience in making PowerPoint slides. The other tasks have the potential to be delegated *if* she can find people to do them.

Do you ever find yourself in Helen's situation? This chapter will help you by explaining the second step of the delegating process: identifying the right people for work you can legitimately delegate. The

FIGURE 2-1. HELEN'S TO-DO LIST.

Task	
Make hotel reservations for new sales personnel.	
Reserve conference room and arrange for audiovisual support, refreshments, and lunches.	
Recruit managers from national sales, marketing, sales support, finance, and product development to speak to the group and participate in luncheons and events.	Me
Prepare PowerPoint presentation.	Me and _____ ?
Prepare agenda for each day's meeting.	Me
Create information packets for each participant.	
Arrange for tickets and transportation to evening baseball game.	

choice is important. To avoid a disappointing outcome, you must delegate to a person who has the following characteristics:

- Time available
- Interest in the task
- Capability and reliability
- Closeness to the problem or issue
- Potential to benefit from the assignment

TIME AVAILABLE

Usually the first thing you need to do in finding the right person is to determine whether that person has enough time. There's no point in loading more work on someone who's already operating at full capacity; doing so guarantees a bad outcome. You might make an exception if the person is uniquely qualified for an assignment—for example, if he or she is the *only* employee who knows how to build sensitivity analysis into a spreadsheet forecast. In a case such as that, you might have to reassign some of the person's regular work to another employee, which could be tricky.

In other cases, you can work with the fully scheduled person if you can reprioritize his or her current assignment. For example:

Helen needs someone to help prepare slides for her orientation meetings—someone who can render Helen's text and bullet points into eye-catching visuals. The most qualified person in the office is Sheldon, a true wizard with PowerPoint and other graphics programs.

Sheldon's calendar, unfortunately, is filled with other commitments. A brief conversation between the two, however, reveals that Sheldon can delay one of his assignments for several weeks, creating time for Helen's request. By reprioritizing his work, he is able to help Helen when she needs his assistance.

Take a look around your workplace the next time you have a job to delegate. Are some people overloaded while others appear to have time on their hands? Is someone working on something that has a lower priority than the task you need to get done? Let your observations guide you to the right people.

. . . .

BEWARE THE PERSON WHO CAN'T SAY NO

Do have a coworker who simply can't say no to an interesting assignment, or to a request from someone else? When the boss asks for a volunteer and everyone begins looking at their shoes, is there a person who always breaks the ice, saying, "Okay, I'll take care of it"? A willingness to pitch in when help is needed is an excellent trait in a coworker or an employee. Just be careful. In his eagerness to please and to help the group, the person who can't say no often overloads himself, with the result that the work is either late or done haphazardly.

. . . .

INTEREST IN THE TASK

A person who finds a prospective task interesting is more likely to take it seriously and do it well, other factors being equal, than a disinterested person. Animated by her interest, she is also more likely to find a way to work the job into her schedule. You can determine a person's interest by asking directly or by intuiting it, based on what you already know about that person. A person like Sheldon, for example, might be interested in developing slides for Helen because:

➤   He enjoys being recognized for his computer graphics skills.

➤   He's bored by all the spreadsheet work he does every day and finds slide development a creative diversion.

➤   He's learned some new PowerPoint tricks that he'd like to test.

In the absence of genuine interest by a delegation candidate, you may be able to generate it through the way you pitch the project. In other words, see if you can make it personally appealing. For example, you might say:

> "I think that you'll learn a lot from this assignment."

> "This assignment will put you in contact with several important people in corporate headquarters. Those contacts might be beneficial to your career."

> "I'm authorized to give you a day of comp time in return for your participation, which will require you to put in some extra hours this week. With the holidays coming up, you might enjoy having an extra day off."

You may also be able to generate interest through your design of the task—that is, by designing the job in a way that naturally appeals to a particular person. For example:

Sarah has a job she'd like to delegate to her staff. The job requires analysis of sales data in two states and development of a full report on the data. As Sarah sees it, two skills or interests are needed: analytical and communications. It's rare to find one person who can or would want to do both. Fortunately, Sarah has one direct report, Herb, who's a terrific numbers guy, and another, Ellen, who has a way with words and really enjoys writing reports. Herb says that he'd like to handle the data analysis and Ellen is eager to show off her report-writing skills. Sarah is able to divide the job into two discrete tasks that she can delegate separately to individuals with different skills and interests. Problem solved!

CAPABILITY AND RELIABILITY

Because delegators bear the ultimate responsibility for tasks they assign to others, *capability* and *reliability* are two magic words you must remember. Your delegation candidate should be fully able to handle the job. Generally, past performance is the best evidence of capability. If Bob has demonstrated his ability to successfully handle a similar assignment in the past and Harold has the *potential* to do the job well, then Bob is the better candidate. Proven ability always trumps potential when you're depending on successful execution, other factors being equal. Reliability is likewise important, because a capable person who isn't reliable may leave you with egg on your face. Look for a candidate with both qualities. If you cannot find that person, look for a reliable person who can be coached or trained in a timely way to the competency level required for the job.

For small assignments, especially those that won't become part of the workplace routine, some direct coaching by you or someone else (yes, coaching jobs can also be delegated) may be all that's needed, as in this example:

"Thanks for agreeing to work this assignment into your schedule, Robin," says Jennifer. "As I mentioned, we want to verify the quality of our packaging supplier. Specifically, we need to ensure that our electric boat pumps are being packaged according to specs and safe from breakage during shipping. Do you follow me so far?"

"Got it," Robin responds.

"Good," says Jennifer. "Your job will be to open and inspect one randomly selected box from each of the fifty cartons that arrive by truck tomorrow. I have one such box here, and I'll demonstrate the three steps of the inspection process. Okay?"

"I'm with you so far."

Once Jennifer has demonstrated the process, she hands another unopened box to Robin, saying, "Okay, now you try it."

This type of personal hands-on coaching is often quick and effective. We'll have more on coaching methods in the next chapter. For more complex assignments, formal training may be required. Because formal training involves time and money, however, reserve it for large or repeatable assignments. For example:

➤ A team of security analysts sent a junior associate to a one-day training program put on by the vendor of their financial software. Once the associate understood how to use the software, the security analysts delegated certain number-crunching chores to her. These chores were something that she would do several times during the course of the normal week.

➤ Eager to delegate one of his department's routine monthly meetings to his next in command, a production manager asked the HR department to enroll his subordinate in a "Meeting Management and Facilitation" seminar. Once this subordinate finished the course, he would be able to plan and moderate those meetings each month, freeing up his boss's time for other duties.

SPREAD THE WORK AROUND

As you dole out assignments, it's very tempting to keep coming back to your most reliable and willing people. Every work group has one or two members whom the boss can always count on to do the work, do it right, and never complain. It's natural to want to delegate as much as possible to these capable and reliable subordinates. But be careful. Their morale and goodwill will eventually evaporate if they see their coworkers getting the same pay but doing a lot less work. You must maintain equity within the unit. So, try to delegate tasks to your team members as equally as possible. You don't want to burn out your best people.

CLOSENESS TO THE PROBLEM OR ISSUE

Whenever you have a problem or an issue to deal with, it's usually best if the people closest to it provide the solution. Thus, if a department suffers from bad morale, the department manager, working directly through his or her direct reports, is best situated to deal with it—not the CEO, not the vice president of operations, and not the HR department. Likewise, if a customer has a problem, it's always best for the people in direct contact with that customer—the sales representative or after-sales service person—to come up with a solution. The reason for empowering people close to the problem is that they almost always have a more intimate understanding of the facts and interpersonal nuances—perhaps better than yours—*and* they have a direct stake in the outcome.

So when you begin looking for people to handle a problem or an issue, consider who is closest to the matter in the course of their normal work.

. . . .

EMPOWER YOUR PEOPLE

The idea of empowering the people closest to problems and giving them appropriate decision-making authority once reserved for managers is a relatively new idea in organizations, but one that usually pays off.

Employee empowerment refers to a workplace culture that gives subordinates substantial discretion in how they accomplish their objectives. Managers tell them what needs to be done but leave it up to them to find the best way to do it. Empowered employees are also given greater authority over company resources. For example, an employee who deals directly with customers may be authorized—without first checking with her boss—to give discounts, refunds, or other services in order to resolve problems or correct errors on the spot. No need to check for the boss's approval. Research suggests that empowerment contributes to greater initiative, motivation, and workplace satisfaction and commitment among employees.

Employee empowerment stands in sharp contrast to *command-and-control* management, a model of management in which information relative to customers and operations flows upward through the chain of command to the top, where decisions are made. Directives based on those decisions are then communicated downward through the same chain of command. This top-down approach to management does *not* inspire a high level of employee commitment and collaboration.

How empowered are your people?

. . . .

POTENTIAL TO BENEFIT FROM THE ASSIGNMENT

Although the primary goal of delegating must be to get a job done *right* and on *time,* you should, when possible, use delegation as a means of expanding the capabilities of subordinates.

Many forward-looking companies put a high value on human capital. For them, the knowledge and skills of their people are worth more than the collective worth of their cash, buildings, equipment, production lines, and other tangible assets. Consider a high-tech start-up enterprise that employs dozens of experienced engineers and scientists. If these people were to walk out the door, the company would have almost nothing of real value.

Companies that value human capital expect managers to use training, coaching, progressive assignments, and other means to nurture and increase the value of the human assets under their control. So, as you try to connect tasks with people, be especially mindful of who would benefit from the experience. Consider both short- and long-term (career) benefits, as in this example:

Tony values Cynthia as an employee. She is bright, hardworking, and reliable. "She's my most promotable subordinate," Tony tells his own boss. "She could be ready for a larger role in the company in two or three years." Tony hates the thought of losing Cynthia as a member of his team, but he accepts the idea that developing talent is part of his job.

In working with Cynthia, Tony keeps his eyes open for assignments that will give her experience or skill-building opportunities in areas where she is weak. Group leadership, in Tony's view, is one of those areas. She has a tendency to fade to the background during group activities. With that in mind, Tony delegates the role of chairperson of the department's process improvement committee to Cynthia. "You understand all the issues," he tells her. "I want you to coordinate the agenda, make sure that all the right people participate, and lead those meetings. It will give you valuable experience—experience that will serve you well as you move up in the company. Are you interested?"

Do you have subordinates like Cynthia—good people who would benefit from the challenge of new assignments? Make a mental note of them, and of what type of assignments would broaden their understanding of the business and help them develop new skills.

QUESTIONS TO ASK YOURSELF

Beyond the five main issues just discussed, get answers to the following questions before selecting a person for an assignment:

➤ How well does the person understand the content of the assignment?

➤ How much training or coaching, if any, will be required?

➤ To what degree is the assignment aligned with the person's workplace goals or interests?

➤ Would the person's other work obligations suffer because of this assignment?

EXERCISE

Using the worksheet in Figure 2-2 as a guide, list three of your current subordinates. Then, as in the example given, identify a task each could handle today with appropriate guidance or preparation.

Once you've identified good candidates for delegated assignments, you're ready for the next step of the process: actually assigning the task. We'll pick up on that step in the next chapter.

FIGURE 2-2. WORKSHEET FOR IDENTIFYING TASKS YOUR SUBORDINATES COULD DO.

Subordinate	Tasks I could delegate		
Cynthia	*Organize and chair monthly process improvement meetings.*	Has time Is interested Is capable/reliable Is close to the problem Would benefit	Yes ___ No ✓ Yes ✓ No ___ Yes ✓ No ___ Yes ✓ No ___ Yes ✓ No ___
1.		Has time Is interested Is capable/reliable Is close to the problem Would benefit	Yes ___ No ___ Yes ___ No ___ Yes ___ No ___ Yes ___ No ___ Yes ___ No ___
2.		Has time Is interested Is capable/reliable Is close to the problem Would benefit	Yes ___ No ___ Yes ___ No ___ Yes ___ No ___ Yes ___ No ___ Yes ___ No ___
3.		Has time Is interested Is capable/reliable Is close to the problem Would benefit	Yes ___ No ___ Yes ___ No ___ Yes ___ No ___ Yes ___ No ___ Yes ___ No ___

CHAPTER REVIEW

Try the following open-book review quiz to find out how much you've learned in this chapter:

1. Assuming that the one person capable of handling a job for you is already fully booked, what tactic might you use to create free space in his or her calendar?

_____

_____

_____

_____

_____

2. What is the best predictor of a person's ability to successfully do a particular job?

_____

_____

_____

_____

3. Why are people closest to a problem or an issue more likely than others to provide a good solution?

_____

_____

_____

_____

_____

4. How might delegated assignments benefit a particular employee?

_____

_____

_____

_____

_____

CHAPTER 3

ASSIGN THE TASK

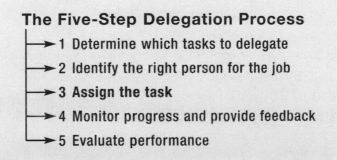

The Five-Step Delegation Process

➤ 1 Determine which tasks to delegate

➤ 2 Identify the right person for the job

➤ 3 **Assign the task**

➤ 4 Monitor progress and provide feedback

➤ 5 Evaluate performance

Your goal in this third step of the process is to define and assign the task to the person you have selected. To effectively pass a task on to an employee, you must ensure that the person you delegate to:

➤ Knows what you want—the desired outcome

➤ Understands how to do the task

➤ Understands how the task fits into the larger picture

➤ Is given sufficient authority and resources to succeed

➤ Is motivated to do a good job

➤ Formally accepts responsibility

The proper method for assigning a delegated task is no different from the method you already use to assign tasks within a person's official job description. Both depend on communication of key information, discussion of any questions, checking for understanding, and agreement on deliverables and deadlines. A "how to do it" demonstration may also be necessary in some cases. The assignment of a new task should begin with a "big picture" explanation—how the task fits in with larger goals of the unit—and end with the employee's clear affirmative acceptance of the task and the responsibilities that go with it.

EXPLAIN THE BIG PICTURE— AND THE PERSONAL BENEFIT

Providing an overview of the job is the best way to begin explaining the assignment. Once people see the big picture—including the job's contribution to your unit's key goals and to their career growth—they will be prepared to listen for the details and ask intelligent questions. Here's an example of a boss explaining the big picture:

> "This job will put you in charge of ordering supplies for the entire department. It's an important responsibility. Having supplies on hand when people need them prevents wasteful slowdowns and keeps our projects on schedule, a key departmental goal. Remember when we ran out of toner cartridges for the color printer right before the board meeting? That caused a lot of anxiety and we had to pay a printing company for a rushed job. At the same time, we need to balance our supply inventory with budget and space constraints. In other words, we have to keep enough supplies on hand to meet anticipated needs, but not so many that we

have to build a new storage room. It's a balancing act that I'll expect you to master. You'll need to communicate with others to understand their upcoming needs, too."

MAKE THE LINK TO GOALS CLEAR

Managers should use every available opportunity to remind people of their unit's key goals: during performance reviews, at staff meetings, during informal conversations, *and* whenever they delegate an assignment. Once people have those goals embedded in their conscious and unconscious minds, they will need much less supervision. They will automatically align their activities and decisions with those goals. Even better, they will identify and eliminate work and processes that contribute little or nothing to the unit's goals: "Boss, we've been completing this monthly report for as long as I can remember. I just don't see what the report contributes to our goal. Does anybody read it? Can we eliminate it?"

How often do you talk to your people about unit goals? If you ask them to state your three top goals, how many people could do so?

It's a good idea to check for understanding at key parts of the assignment communication—and this is one of them. "So, Alice, do you see why it's important to have the right level of supplies available?" At this point, try to keep the discussion at the top level; the details can come later. Give a general description of what success would look like:

"In the ideal situation, you'll provide the supplies we need when we need them, but with a minimum of excess inventory. If we keep supplies at just the right level, our costs will stay in line with our budget expenses over the course of the year, and you know how important cost control is these days! The more you understand present and future supply needs, the better you'll be able to do this."

MOTIVATE AS YOU ASSIGN THE JOB

As you communicate the big picture and ideal outcome, add a dose of motivation. Make it clear how accepting the challenge and doing a good job will benefit the person taking on the job:

"Alice, this job will add to your normal workload, but you're a very organized person. I'm confident that you'll find a way to handle it. I'm also confident that you'll benefit from the experience. By managing the stockroom, you'll get a better understanding of the work of the whole department. Taking on new responsibilities, figuring out how to get things done, overcoming obstacles—this is how we grow and advance in our careers. And I think you'll find this assignment an interesting change of pace from your routine."

For some people—people like Alice—increased responsibility and challenge are motivating. Don't you wish that most of your direct reports were like them? Just aim them in the right direction, provide appropriate resources, flip the "on" switch, and let them go. Unfortunately, not everyone is motivated by increased responsibility and challenge—at least by the type you have to offer. So, what can you do to motivate them? Money can be a motivator, at least in the short term, but don't attach pay increases or bonuses to delegated tasks. Fortunately, other motivators are available:

➢ **Recognition.** This is a basic human need. When people see their peers being recognized for making an extra effort or doing good work, they want to be recognized as well. So, compliment people whenever you see them doing something well. And be public about it.

➢ **Empowerment.** People also innately crave empowerment. They want to feel some control over their lives and their work. Consequently, you should involve subordinates whenever practical in decisions that affect them (e.g., "What do you think is the best way to do this?"). That way, they will be working as much for themselves as for you when they take on an added assignment.

➢ **Ownership.** Have you ever had an assembly-line job where you attached a part or slapped a label on every item that passed down the line? Since it requires little if any thinking, creativity, or decision making, workers feel like cogs in a piece of machinery and become alienated from their work. Many of the tasks that non-assembly-line employees are given have this same characteristic. It may be possible to avoid this problem by delegating "whole" jobs. A whole job is one for which a person takes start-to-finish responsibility—he or she "owns" that task and its outcome. You must, however, take care that in structuring the assignment you're delegating only what the person is capable of doing well. You don't want to set the person up for failure! In some cases, therefore, it makes sense to break up difficult or complex whole jobs into their coherent parts and then delegate each to a person who is capable of executing it successfully.

Implement these motivation tools and you'll find that people will perform their delegated tasks in a more satisfactory manner.

FILL IN THE DETAILS

Once a person understands the big picture, he or she will want to learn exactly what must be done. This creates a natural transition to the next part of the assignment dialogue: explaining the details. In some cases, you may want the person to follow a prescribed set of steps:

> "I've always used a checklist approach to keeping track of supply needs. Every Monday I check the inventory of twenty-eight key supplies against our official reorder point quantities. Then I

ask the production manager if he'll have any special needs for the next two weeks. Then I order what we need. Once you see my file, you'll understand what I mean and you'll be able to continue that method."

A by-the-numbers approach to communicating the task gives you an opportunity to walk the person through each required step, coaching and checking for understanding as you go.

Alternatively, you may leave it up to the person to create his or her own approach. This method requires the person to think, to stretch, and to take greater ownership of the assigned task. However, if you follow this method, it's smart to ask for an action plan; doing so will give you some assurance that the person will get off to a good start:

"I'm perfectly happy to let you create your own approach to this task. After all, it will be your responsibility. But let's review your action plan together before you begin."

FROM THE HISTORY BOOKS

The World War II Battle of Midway (June 4, 1942) resulted in a lopsided victory for the U.S. Navy, which in this episode was led by a delegated commander. A week or so before the event, the American commander in Hawaii, Admiral William Halsey, was hospitalized and unable to lead his forces—two carrier task forces—in a bold mission to intercept and engage the Imperial Japanese Navy, which American code breakers had discovered to be steaming toward an assault on Midway Island. From his hospital bed, Halsey delegated command of the operation to Rear Admiral Ray Spruance. Spruance was new to carrier warfare; his experience up to that time had been in heavy cruisers. But his reputation for intelligence and calmness under pressure gave his boss confidence that he could handle the job. Halsey hedged his bet by appointing Rear Admiral Frank

Fletcher, an experienced carrier officer, as Spruance's second in command.

Because he had little solid information about the opposing force, Halsey didn't try to micromanage Spruance's operation. Instead, he gave him and Fletcher very general instructions, leaving all tactical decisions in their hands: "Be governed by the principle of calculated risk," he told them, "which you shall interpret to mean the avoidance of exposure of your force to superior enemy forces without good prospects of inflicting greater damage on them."*

Halsey's decision to empower his subordinates was wise. The location, direction of travel, and composition of the opposing force were unknown at the time. Spruance and Fletcher would have to handle the situation as it unfolded. Their decisions, and luck, produced a disaster for the Imperial Japanese Navy and marked the turning point in the war in the Pacific.

Lesson: The more ambiguous the situation, the greater amount of decision-making authority and flexibility you may have to give to your subordinates. Just be sure that you have a high level of trust in the people who will make those decisions.

. . . .

Discuss Resource Support

As you reveal the details of an assignment, also indicate the extent to which resource support will be provided. Resource support may include any of the following:

➢ A budget

➢ Other helping hands (e.g., tech support, someone to do data entry)

➢ Materials or machine time

➢ Training

*Admiral William Halsey as quoted in Samuel Eliot Morison, *History of United States Naval Operations in World War II*, Vol. 4 (Boston: Little Brown, 1947), 84.

The level of resource support should be determined by the requirements of the work. It makes no sense to ask someone to do a job and then fail to provide sufficient resources to complete it successfully. Discuss necessary resources with your subordinate; he or she may be aware of needs you may not have considered, or may have ideas on resources that can be tapped:

> "Alice, besides having John to help you restock the supplies monthly, what other help will you need on this project?"
>
> "Well, I just saw an announcement about a negotiating course that HR is offering next week. I think better negotiating skills would help me deal with the vendors; shall I sign up for it?"

Provide Authority and Decision-Making Power

Support should also include an appropriate level of authority and decision-making power. Many managers are tightfisted in providing these out of fear they will lose control or diminish their own organizational power. However, you cannot make someone responsible for a job without giving that person a commensurate level of authority and decision-making power. If you withhold these, the person will either fail to complete the job or be forced to run to you with every problem and every decision—which means the job will come right back to you!

> "Alice, I've increased your spending authority to $5,000, the average monthly invoice from our largest supplier. And I've alerted the staff that they should submit their requests for special items to you. You'll need to work out a system that works for all concerned."

. . . .

TIP

BE MORE SPECIFIC ABOUT OUTCOMES THAN MEANS

To the extent possible, specify the job more in terms of the outcome you desire and less in terms of the means to that end. Consider what would happen if you gave your subordinate this instruction: "Reorder supplies by 10:00 every Friday." Even if she complied, you might run out of supplies between orders. Now consider if your instruction was this: "Reorder supplies so that we have what we need when we need it." Given that outcome-oriented instruction, a resourceful subordinate would make certain that you never ran out of supplies.

Giving more attention to desired outcomes than to means requires giving greater autonomy to another person. If that makes you uncomfortable, you may be overly controlling as a boss. Just remember, if you want to get certain jobs out of your hair—and also develop the competencies of your people—you must be willing to transfer some level of decision-making authority with delegated tasks.

. . . .

BE SPECIFIC ABOUT THE OUTCOME YOU EXPECT

Have you ever spent an entire day doing something for your boss only to be told, "That's *not* what I wanted"? If you have, you probably felt like saying, "Well, why didn't you tell me what you wanted! Do you think I'm a mind reader?"

Failure to clearly communicate the desired end result may be the biggest source of disappointment and angst in delegation situations. As a delegator, it's your responsibility to spell out what you want— what success will look like. Don't expect other people to read your mind.

ENTERTAIN QUESTIONS

Your subordinate is likely to have questions about the assignment and the results you expect:

"Who has the information on this?"

"Where is the file?"

"Do you want this information presented as a spreadsheet, or as a report?"

"Can you help me with _____?"

"Can I share part of this task with _____?"

"I'm not certain that I can get it done by Friday. Would next Wednesday be okay?"

Questions are useful in that they surface details you may have forgotten to communicate. They give the person an opportunity to ask for those overlooked details and to confirm his own understanding of your wishes. If he isn't asking questions, take that as a warning sign. He either is resistant to accept the job, is too reserved to ask for the information he needs, or is simply not thinking about the job or how he'll handle it. If questions aren't asked, initiate dialogue by asking a few questions of your own:

"What problems do you foresee?"

"Am I asking for more than you can handle right now? What do you need to off-load or postpone?"

"Is Friday a reasonable deadline to expect this to be completed?"

"Do you have ideas on how to improve this even more?"

"What would you do if _____ happened?"

"How do you feel about taking on this assignment?"

The point of the question-and-answer session is to surface and address whatever might stand between your subordinate and the successful completion of a delegated task. The Q&A session also provides an opportunity for both of you to brainstorm different approaches to the job.

GET AGREEMENT ON DELIVERABLES AND DEADLINES

Obtaining agreement is an important element of effective management. Whether you're talking to someone about her goals for the coming year or about a task you'd like her to accept, her verbal agreement is very important. By agreeing, she makes a commitment and accepts personal responsibility for certain stated deliverables.

As you seek agreement, focus on specific outcomes and, if appropriate, the stated deadline:

> "Then I can count on you to make all the travel and hotel arrangements for the summer sales meeting by April 20, and communicate them to the team by May 1, right?"
>
> "Yes. I'll commit to that."

Complex Assignments Need Formal Schedules

You may find that some people need help in keeping on track toward your deadline, even though they've agreed to it and have it marked on their calendars. Especially for large, complex assignments, they need to "pace" their work in a way that everything will be satisfactorily completed when the calendar date arrives. For example, if they delay starting work on the project too long, or save too much of the work for the last few days, they may be unable to meet your deadline.

If you suspect this may be a problem (and every large and complex assignment is a candidate for problems), ask the subordinate to create a written work plan or work schedule. One of the simplest to construct is a Gantt chart, a bar chart that lists the component parts of the task in the left-hand column, and when they should begin and end in columns

FIGURE 3-1. EXAMPLE GANTT CHART.

Task Components	3/1–3/5	3/8–3/12	3/15–3/19	3/22–3/26
Develop draft of plan.	XXXXX			
Circulate plan for comment.		XXXXX		
Finalize plan.			XXXXX	
Prepare to implement.				XXXXX

to the right. For example, the Gantt chart depicted in Figure 3-1 lays out a plan that a direct report has prepared for moving the department office to a new location in the building. As requested by her manager, she has identified all key components of the task as well as weekly periods in which each component should be begun and completed. Their discussion around assignment of the task would include all the things that must go into the plan, the sequence of task components, and the reasonableness of the schedule itself.

In this simple example, the task follows a strictly linear progression: First create a plan draft, then have it reviewed by key participants, then finalize it, then implement it, *in that order*. Each step depends on the completion of the one before it. Review of the draft plan, for example, cannot begin until the plan is actually drafted!

Not every complex task is so linear. In a more complex version of this case, for instance, the subordinate might be asked to work in parallel with the interior designer to plan the renovation of the space the department will move to in the building. Thus, the subordinate would have to deal with two sets of related activities in tandem. These complications need to be reflected in the schedule.

Build Checkpoints into the Assignment

While you're on the subject of deadlines, agreement on a long-term project should include periodic checkpoints as a means of ensuring progress. Checkpoints give the manager an opportunity to periodically observe progress, identify developing problems, and maintain control over a delegated task for which he or she bears the ultimate responsibility without looking over the employee's shoulder in a way that defeats the purpose of delegation. Checkpoints give the manager confidence.

This chapter has described the things you must think about and communicate when delegating an assignment. How well you pass on this information to your subordinates will shape the outcome. To help you remember what you need to communicate, we've created a simple checklist (see Figure 3-2). Use it the next few times you prepare to delegate tasks. Before you know it, you'll be automatically communicating this information when delegating assignments.

FIGURE 3-2. ASSIGNMENT CHECKLIST.

☐ **The Big Picture** *How does the assignment contribute to large goals?*
☐ **Key Details** *What essential details should you communicate?*
☐ **Support** *What material resources or support do you plan to provide?*
☐ **Authority** *How will you make sure the employee has the authority to succeed at the task?*
☐ **Outcome** *What results do you expect the employee to deliver?*
☐ **Deadline and Checkpoints** *Do you have a deadline in mind? What are the logical points at which you should check progress?*

CHAPTER REVIEW

Try the following open-book review quiz to find out how much you've learned in this chapter:

1. Why is it important to first communicate the big picture and how the delegated task fits in?

_____

_____

_____

_____

_____

2. Name and explain at least two motivational tools you can use when delegating to others.

_____

_____

_____

_____

_____

3. Cite a situation from your own experience in which the person who was delegated a particular task needed a certain amount of authority and decision-making power in order to get the job done.

_____

_____

_____

_____

_____

4. Why is it important for the person who is taking on a delegated task to verbally agree to do so?

_____

_____

_____

_____

_____

5. How can a Gantt chart be used to schedule long-term and complex assignments?

_____

_____

_____

_____

_____

CHAPTER 4

MONITOR PROGRESS AND PROVIDE FEEDBACK

The Five-Step Delegation Process

1 Determine which tasks to delegate
2 Identify the right person for the job
3 Assign the task
4 Monitor progress and provide feedback
5 Evaluate performance

We're now at the fourth step in the delegating process. Work on the delegated task should now be under way. Your job at this point is to periodically check for progress and problems, and to provide feedback as needed.

As a manager or supervisor, you routinely observe employee performance and provide feedback, coaching, and other support as needed. Your aim is to keep things on track to a successful conclusion. That's part of the "control" function of management. The same applies to delegated tasks, especially those that are newly assigned or unfamiliar to the employees who assumed responsibility for them. If these people become stuck or start going off in the wrong direction, it's best to find out right away and provide advice or assistance that will get them back on track. The earlier you can catch a problem, the more quickly you can apply coaching or other corrective actions. This does *not* imply that you should take back the assigned task at the first sign of trouble; it simply means that you may have to help the employee assigned the task to manage the job more successfully. The last thing you want is for the employee to fail and hand the task back to you. This would result in a double failure: The employee's skill and confidence would not be increased, and the task would be back in your lap.

Except for the most routine tasks, expect some changes from your initial understanding of the delegated assignment. New information may come to light, or new developments may occur that will change the scope or the deadline of the assignment. Monitoring progress keeps you abreast of these changes and gives you an opportunity to address any that may have serious consequences.

MAKE USE OF CHECKPOINTS

We said in the previous chapter that (unless the job is small) you and the person to whom you've delegated a task should agree on a set of checkpoints over the term of the assignment. A *checkpoint* is a predetermined point at which progress will be observed and evaluated. You undoubtedly use checkpoints in the normal course of your work as a manager or supervisor to observe progress and maintain control over operations:

"Send me the initial draft once you've completed it and I'll get back to you with my comments. I'd like that draft by Tuesday afternoon."

"Let's meet every Friday at 4 P.M. to talk about where you are in the project and what needs to be done."

"I want a weekly status update on each of the following activities: _____."

"Once you've organized the list of suppliers, come see me. We'll look it over and move on to the next part of the assignment."

Use checkpoints in the same way with your delegated tasks. Each provides an opportunity to observe progress and to provide feedback, coaching, and motivation as needed. Remember, you retain the ultimate responsibility for tasks you delegate to others. If you don't bother to monitor a delegated task that goes bad, its failure will be partly your fault. You can't wriggle off the hook of failure by telling your boss, "Gee, I asked Sharon to do that job and she let me down." Such excuses will only point out your own failure to delegate wisely and to monitor progress.

MONITOR WITHOUT MICROMANAGING

Finding the right level of monitoring is an art. While it is true that you are responsible for the final success or failure of all tasks in your department, it is also true that you have turned over ownership of delegated tasks. The last thing you want to do is make employees feel that you are looking over their shoulders, checking their work obsessively, and making all the decisions yourself. Gauge each situation carefully, and give the employee as much scope as possible. A casual question or two may be enough to confirm that an experienced and confident employee is on track. You may ask for more formal evidence, such as written plans or reports, in situations in which a less experienced employee is handling a task.

. . . .

MONITORING THE OFF-SITE SUBORDINATE

An estimated 25 percent of U.S. white-collar workers now do some or all of their work at home. Many more spend a portion of the time working at remote locations: client offices, satellite work centers, hotel rooms, airport terminals, and Wi-Fi-enabled coffee shops. Perhaps this describes your own work situation. Are you working from home now and then? Are your subordinates working on the road? Whatever the case, physical distance complicates the manager's need to monitor progress and provide timely feedback because employees cannot be observed directly.

In these situations, you should demonstrate greater interest in results and less concern with *how* those results are produced. Instead of worrying if employees are watching the Golf Channel, you should reach an agreement with them on deliverables, progress checkpoints, and deadlines, then leave it up to the employees to complete the tasks.

Even when people are out of the office, you can still monitor through phone calls, e-mails, and periodic progress reports.

. . . .

PROVIDE FEEDBACK

Scheduled checkpoints are perfect opportunities to provide feedback without appearing to micromanage—something you must avoid doing. *Feedback* refers to a communication process by which output (information) is returned, or "fed back," to its source as a means of regulating the situation. The temperature control mechanism in your home offers a handy example. Using the thermostat on your living room wall as a sensor, your furnace asks, "How warm is the room?" The answer is communicated by the thermostat back to the furnace, which responds. If the room is too cold, the furnace intervenes by sending more heat. Managers use feedback in the same "sense and respond" manner. Figure 4-1 is a graphic example of a "feedback loop," showing communication going from the manager to an employee ("How are things going?"), and then being fed back to the manager ("Fine," or "I'm having trouble with something"). The initial communication, of course, can come from the employee ("I have a problem").

Feedback used to be called "constructive criticism," but that expression captures only a small part of what feedback means. Constructive criticism is a one-way communication in which the listener learns something and the speaker learns nothing. So, as you develop your feedback skills, remember that you must give equal attention to your capacity to give *and* to receive.

FIGURE 4-1. A FEEDBACK LOOP.

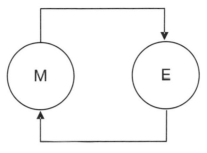

Source: Adapted from Perry McIntosh, Richard Luecke, and Jeffrey H. Davis, *Interpersonal Communications in the Workplace*, 2nd ed. (New York: American Management Association, 2008), 98.

Effective feedback in a workplace setting has several important characteristics:

> **It is descriptive, not judgmental.** A boss trained in giving feedback won't say, "You're not up to the job." Instead, he will describe what he actually sees: "You don't appear to be familiar with using Excel's graphing function to make pie charts." Nor should he presume to understand or pass judgment on a person's motivations when giving feedback: "I don't think you're committed to this project." Being judgmental or presuming a person's motivations will merely put the person in a defensive posture, reducing the effectiveness of communication.

> **It focuses on modifiable behavior.** An experienced boss will give feedback only on those things that the employee can actually change. She won't say, "I think that you have the wrong personality type for this work" or "To design this customer survey well, at a minimum you should have a master's degree in market research." Neither of these are things that the employee can change, at least not in the short run. Contrast these examples to feedback that focuses on modifiable behavior: "If you're having trouble organizing the report, consider making a list of the three or four main things you want to get across to your readers. Then organize the report around them."

➤   **It is specific.** The feedback-savvy boss is very definite and avoids generalizations. Instead of saying, "This report could be better organized," which imparts little useful information, he will say something like this: "You could get your points across more clearly by using the first paragraph to state the problem and suggest possible solutions; then use the following sections to flesh out the details."

➤   **It is well-timed.** As in most endeavors, timing is an important element of effective feedback. Give it as soon after an event or impasse as possible, before memories fade and the employee has moved on to other things. For instance, don't say, "A few weeks ago I noticed that you and Bob had fallen behind schedule. What was the problem?" A few weeks in a fast-moving organization is ancient history. Imagine how much more effective your feedback would be if you said as soon as you realized there was a problem, "I just noticed that you and Bob have fallen behind schedule. What's up?" Also, if the employee is waiting day after day for your feedback, you may be undermining her ability to complete her work on schedule.

➤   **It works in both directions.** Think of feedback as a two-way street, with traffic moving in both directions. If you are simply "telling" someone what you think, it's not real feedback, because there is no information—no signal—coming from the other direction. So encourage the employee to speak freely about the task, about any problems he's experiencing, about deadline concerns, and so forth. And *don't forget to listen.* Give him your full attention and don't interrupt—except for an occasional "I see" or "Tell me more"—while he is stating his case. You will learn nothing and accomplish little if you do all the talking.

If you follow the suggestions given for these five characteristics, you'll have productive feedback sessions with your people. If everything is going well, indicate your praise: "You're doing very well with this. Keep up the good work." If it's a mixed bag, praise those parts of the work that have been done well, and then add a dose of encouragement: "Well, you really nailed the first half of the draft report. I'm confident that you'll bring the second half up to the same high level in no time."

FIGURE 4-2. SCORING SHEET FOR THE FIVE CHARACTERISTICS OF EFFECTIVE FEEDBACK.

	Score (1–5)	Notes
I was descriptive, not judgmental.		
I focused on modifiable behavior.		
I was specific.		
I provided timely feedback.		
I listened as well as talked.		
Total Score Total Score/5 = Average Feedback Rating		

RATE YOUR FEEDBACK

Think back to your most recent experiences in giving feedback to employees. Then using a scoring sheet like the one in Figure 4-2, rate yourself in terms of each of the five characteristics of effective feedback using a scale of 1 to 5, with 1 being poor and 5 being excellent. On your sheet, in the "Notes" column, write down what you did well in delivering the feedback and what you need to improve on. Return to this self-rating exercise periodically until you've made a habit of being very good to excellent for each characteristic.

PROVIDE COACHING

In business organizations, managers and supervisors routinely use coaching to overcome performance problems and to develop the skills of their subordinates. Coaching can be informal and on the spot: "I see that you're having a problem. Can I quickly show you an easy shortcut?" Or it can be given in formally planned doses: "Jake, if you're agreeable, I can team you up with Sherry each of the next three Monday afternoons from four until five. She's a wizard at creating budgets in Excel spreadsheets. Three one-hour sessions with her will bring you up to speed."

Delegate Coaching When You Can

Note that in our previous example the boss isn't going to spend hours coaching Jake on the ins and outs of creating Excel spreadsheets. He has delegated that task to Sherry, one of his subordinates. If you're a manager, you must always be mindful of your time, delegating tasks—including coaching—whenever possible. When you delegate a coaching task, you are telling the person that you respect her know-how. It is a form of praise and appreciation. Can you think of coaching activities that you might be able to delegate to competent subordinates?

The effectiveness of coaching—both formal and informal—is positively correlated with the coached person's motivation to learn and improve. If you have someone who's not interested in self-improvement, the time you spend coaching will have a low payoff. So whenever you are considering coaching someone, weigh the potential for positive results versus little improvement.

An employee who needs coaching should also be at a point in job development where he or she is *prepared* to learn. Anyone who has raised children understands that there is little point in trying to teach certain skills if a child hasn't reached a certain point in his or her cognitive and physical development. For example, in order to read and write, ride a bicycle, climb stairs, and so forth, a child must have already attained an appropriate level of development. We observe something similar in the workplace. A person with no hands-on experience with a personal computer isn't at the point of learning to build financial models on a spreadsheet. A new salesperson isn't at the point of meeting customers and closing deals before he or she understands the product line and competing products. So don't get too far ahead of your subordinate's skill development when you begin coaching.

Avoid Common Mistakes

Your coaching will also be more effective if you avoid two common mistakes: talking too much and listening too little. If you do all the talking, you'll never learn what is impeding the employee's performance, and you'll never know if he or she understands what you're saying. If you fail to listen, you'll miss cues that would focus your coaching on the issues that matter.

NEVER TAKE BACK THE MONKEY

In a classic *Harvard Business Review* article written in the early 1970s, William Oncken Jr. and Donald L. Wass cautioned managers *never* to allow subordinates to "put the monkey" (i.e., the delegated task) back onto their backs whenever problems are encountered. Managers who allow this to happen, they warn, will never be effective delegators. Instead, their time will be eaten up by obligations that properly belong with others.*

Many employees are very skilled at returning "monkeys." They appeal to your sympathy, your vanity, or your fears. For example:

"I've got so much to do this week—I'm just swamped!"

"Gee, you really are a whiz at this. Maybe you should handle it?"

"I'm afraid I'm going to make a mess of this and delay the launch of the product. Could you handle it?"

Yes, it is often faster and easier to "take back the monkey"—to do the job yourself—but resist the urge to do so! You don't want to encourage this behavior.

The monitoring step of the delegating process will put you in regular contact with task owners and their problems. Just remember that they—not you—are the owners and must remain so. You can provide feedback, coaching, and advice and resources, but it's not your job to

---

*William Oncken Jr. and Donald L. Wass, "Management Time: Who's Got the Monkey?" *Harvard Business Review*, November–December 1974.

do work for which *they* have accepted responsibility. When they come to your office to discuss problems, be helpful and supportive, but be sure that they leave with the metaphorical "monkey" still on their back, not on yours.

CHAPTER REVIEW

Try the following open-book review quiz to find out how much you've learned in this chapter:

1. What is a checkpoint and how can managers use checkpoints to monitor the progress of employee assignments?

_____

_____

_____

_____

2. What is the difference between constructive criticism and feedback as described in this chapter?

_____

_____

_____

_____

3. List and explain at least two characteristics of effective feedback.

_____

_____

4. List and comment on two common mistakes that many managers make in coaching employees.

_____

_____

CHAPTER 5

EVALUATE PERFORMANCE

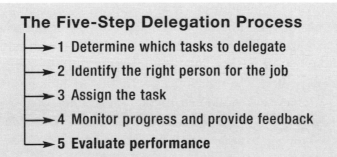

The Five-Step Delegation Process
1 Determine which tasks to delegate
2 Identify the right person for the job
3 Assign the task
4 Monitor progress and provide feedback
5 Evaluate performance

valuation is the final step in the delegation process. Once the task is completed, you should objectively evaluate how well it was done. This can be done quickly and informally for small delegated tasks, or more formally for bigger assignments.

Evaluation takes time—probably your most limited commodity—but for several reasons it is time well spent. First, the person who did the work deserves to know how well she did on the assignment.

Acknowledging a job well done provides important psychic rewards and reinforces good performance. If the person fell short in some way, she needs to know not only where she was inadequate in carrying out the job but also how her future performance can be improved. Second, as a manager, you need to know as much as possible about your subordinate's capabilities so that you can delegate tasks accordingly. A fact-based evaluation will indicate the following:

> Something about the person's strengths and weaknesses that would otherwise pass unnoticed; the assignment of a new task will often surface these strengths and weaknesses.

> Where employee training or development may be needed.

> The types of assignments the person is prepared to take on in the future.

Performance evaluation (review or "appraisal") is widely practiced in both for-profit and not-for-profit organizations, for the reasons just stated and to make decisions on promotions, bonuses, and career development. Evaluation of individual employees is typically done annually and considers all of the individual's activities, including interactions with customers and nondepartmental personnel. A performance record is created and filed in the HR department. When we evaluate how well someone handled a delegated task, however, the scope, purpose, and formality of appraisal are naturally more limited. Therefore, if you're already seasoned in giving annual performance reviews, this last step should be easily handled.

It's temptingly easy to overlook this last important step or to give it inadequate attention. The delegated task has been done, and there are many more things to do. Who has time to analyze the finished task and provide feedback to the employee? You have more than enough pressing matters on your desk, right? If you want to become a master delegator, however—and if you want employees to become better performers—take the time to evaluate and give feedback.

FOCUS ON RESULTS

As you conduct your evaluation, focus on results. In most cases, *what* was accomplished is more important than *how* it was accomplished (except when it comes to matters of safety and workplace rules). In fact, if a person has found a better way to do something within the bounds of acceptable behavior, he should get positive strokes for using initiative and creativity.

Your evaluation, above all, should be *based on facts* gathered through direct observation. Never base your evaluation on hearsay. If you're not in a position to fully evaluate the person's performance—for example, if you're wondering how well the person was able to collaborate with teammates or satisfy a customer problem—make quiet inquiries of others who can give you an objective, fact-based appraisal.

In most instances, you can limit your evaluation of delegated tasks to three main areas: completeness, timeliness, and quality.

Was the Task Complete?

When you first assigned the task, you should have been very clear and detailed in your expectations for results. If you did that, the employee should have had no trouble knowing what the completed job would look like. And you should have no trouble recognizing whether the job was complete or only partially done.

If the job was not completed, determine the cause, beginning with yourself. Look back on the episode and ask yourself and the employee the following questions:

"Were my instructions unclear?"

"Did I provide inadequate resources?"

"Was my deadline unreasonable?"

"Did I assume too much about the employee's [your] capabilities?"

"Did I fail to coach when needed?"

If you answered "yes" to any of these questions, make a mental note to be more careful when delegating and overseeing future tasks. If the fault wasn't yours, determine why the employee failed. Understanding the cause is the first step toward corrective action.

Sometimes an assignment changes during the course of its completion for reasons that have little to do with your instructions or the employee's skills. Conditions change and requirements evolve. You should keep abreast of these developments as you monitor projects.

In any case, don't accept incomplete work. Doing so merely puts the monkey back on your back, thereby defeating your purpose in delegating the work.

Was the Task Completed on Time?

A properly delegated task has a deadline, such as "by this time next week" or "by close of business tomorrow." If your deadline was reasonable, that deadline should have been met. If it wasn't met, determine the cause of the delay. Were there extenuating circumstances over which the assignee had no control? Did you underestimate the magnitude of the task or was the person simply lax in completing the work? Again, what you learn through evaluation will help you and the employee to better understand yourselves and to improve future performance.

. . . .

 DON'T UNDERESTIMATE THE TIME REQUIREMENT

It's often easy to underestimate the time a subordinate will need to complete a job. If you've done the job yourself dozens of time, you may think, "Well, it shouldn't take more than four hours—that's how long it takes me." Remember that it may take longer for your subordinate to do the job, either because he's unfamiliar with it or because he lacks your skills and experience. Any task done for the first time, whether it's a household chore or an office assignment, takes longer. Economists have formalized that intuitively obvious fact into the concept of the "experience curve." So factor those differences into time estimates for delegated tasks.

. . . .

Does the Task Meet Quality Standards?

In delegating the task, you should have specified the level of quality you required, such as "a clearly written report with no typos covering all three contract issues" or "a list of no fewer than five qualified parts suppliers, with a brief assessment of each vendor's strengths and weaknesses." Quality may have measurable and nonmeasurable components.

Quality is important because every task you accept—delegated or otherwise—contributes to your "brand" as a manager. *By thy quality they will know thee.* If you routinely accept half-baked work, you'll develop a reputation as a half-baked manager in charge of a unit with low standards. Your subordinates will see a low threshold of performance as acceptable and normal. However, if you set the bar of quality high and enforce high standards, you'll develop a more flattering reputation, and people will learn to work up to the elevated standard you expect.

. . . .

 ### SET THE BAR THROUGH EXAMPLE

Whether you recognize it or not, your own work performance sets the quality standard for the unit. If your work is unremarkable and typically behind schedule, people will notice and model their behavior accordingly. Conversely, if your work is excellent and prompt, and if you always do what you say you'll do, most people will adopt your standard and incorporate it into the work they do for you.

. . . .

If the quality of a delegated task does not meet your specified standard, don't allow it to slide by. Instead, sit down with the employee, identify shortcomings, and determine what can be done to bring the work up to specifications. Give the person a chance to create a remediation plan. If she is responsible for the work, it's also her responsibility (and privilege) to find a solution. Give her a chance to rise to the challenge.

One final remark on quality: It may not be necessary for the person to do the job as well as you would do it. You might be capable of writing a report at a Pulitzer Prize level of quality, but that level of quality may be unnecessary. As the old saying goes, Don't allow the perfect to get in the way of the good.

. . . .

OTHER EVALUATION CRITERIA

For a delegated task, we generally evaluate performance on only the three criteria already covered: completeness, timeliness, and quality. However, as a manager you should use every opportunity to assess the strengths and weaknesses of subordinates more broadly. The better you understand these strengths and weaknesses, the better the decisions you'll make with respect to promotions, bonuses, career development, and future assignments. So make both mental and file notes about other aspects of performance on delegated tasks. These might include:

- ➤ Adaptability
- ➤ Effective use of resources
- ➤ Ability to prioritize
- ➤ Self-motivation
- ➤ Initiative and creativity
- ➤ Ability to collaborate with others
- ➤ Communication skills
- ➤ Problem-solving ability
- ➤ Ability to lead without formal authority
- ➤ Professionalism

. . . .

BEWARE OF PITFALLS IN EVALUATING PERFORMANCE

Whether you are evaluating an employee's performance of an ad hoc delegated task or of an entire year's effort, beware of the following three psychological errors that managers often make: the halo effect, isolated incident bias, and personal difference bias.

The Halo Effect

The *halo effect* is an unconscious cognitive bias that allows our judgment of a person in one category to carry over to another, unrelated category. For example, if you've always found Judy's work with customers to be especially good, you might be tempted to think that her work with peers is equally good even when you have no evidence to support that view. The converse is also possible: Once we begin thinking of a particular employee as a loser, we may be unwilling to recognize that person's good work even when we see it. Thus, we must be careful in evaluating the different dimensions of a person's work.

Isolated Incident Bias

Have you ever allowed a person's failure or poor performance in one instance to shape your entire perception of that person? "Bill submitted his proposal two weeks later than promised. I guess he's unreliable." This is an example of *isolated instance bias*. True, Bill's work in this one situation was late, but the totality of Bill's work might justify the opposite view of his reliability.

Because so many delegated tasks are themselves isolated incidents, be especially wary of this evaluation bias.

Personal Difference Bias

People have a natural tendency to be more accepting of individuals who resemble them—by race, religion, educational background, political beliefs, gender, and so forth—and less accepting of people whom they perceive as "different." This is called *personal difference bias*. Have you ever felt a special bond with someone who grew up in your town or who attended your school—a bond that you do not feel toward other people? This is what we're talking about. And it can affect how you view a person's performance unless you resist it.

Tribalism may be baked into our DNA, but it's not an excuse for being nonobjective when evaluating the work of others. We can rise above it. Managers have an obligation to put aside personal bias and evaluate everyone and everyone's work with disciplined objectivity. This isn't difficult once we realize that most individual differences are superficial. In fact, people of different races, religions, and cultures have much more in common than not.

COMMUNICATE YOUR EVALUATION TO THE EMPLOYEE

Communication is the capstone of performance evaluation. After-action discussion with a subordinate provides you with one of your best opportunities to motivate, advise, and direct your people. This is something you need to handle extremely well.

Be Specific in Your Praise

If your evaluation is positive, congratulate the person on a job well done. And don't be reluctant to say, "Thanks! That was good work." Saying thanks costs you nothing yet can be a powerful motivator. But go a step further. Specify aspects of job performance that were particularly well done. Instead of saying, "You did a very good job with that presentation to the sales staff," point to the specific things that merit praise:

> You did a very good job with that presentation to the sales staff, Joanne. You used your PowerPoint slides very effectively. Lots of people make the mistake of simply reading the text in the slides to the audience, as if the audience doesn't know how to read

what's on the screen. And moving away from the podium, as you did, and engaging individual members of the audience kept them alert and involved.

Pointing out specific aspects of good performance encourages people to repeat those particular actions in the future.

ADDRESS PEOPLE'S SHORTCOMINGS

Not every delegated task will be done right, or entirely right. When you find a gap between what you had a right to expect and the actual performance, make it the focus of your discussion with the employee. Some managers accept half-baked work rather than confront employees with uncomfortable discussions about their shortcomings. Yes, having to tell people that their work is subpar is an unpleasant experience, but it must be done. Doing otherwise simply reinforces the idea that substandard performance is acceptable to you.

You can reduce the discomfort of these discussions by beginning on a positive note—by recognizing aspects of the job that the person did well. Doing so will help to forestall defensiveness on the employee's part. Then move on to performance gaps. Here are a few tips for handling these discussions:

> **Keep it fact based.** If you stick to observable facts that neither party can deny, your employee cannot feel that you are simply venting your personal displeasure or expressing a personal opinion: "Your work was fine, but we agreed that it would be finished last week, not this morning. Am I right?"

> **Focus on the problem, not the person.** Don't say, "You're not taking this work seriously." That would be a personal attack based on a guess by you. For all you know, the employee may have a perfectly good reason for delivering the job late—a reason that you do not yet understand. So, say something that focuses on the problem instead: "Being on time matters. What caused the delay?"

➤ **Put the problem in a larger context.** Explain why the problem is important to you and to the work group: "Last week's deadline wasn't arbitrary; I didn't pull it out of thin air. We needed your report last week in order to get the project team working on its recommendations. They couldn't begin their work until they had your full report. Being a week late has put them into a time bind."

➤ **Get the employee talking about the performance problem and its cause.** Effective feedback depends on two-way communication. Encourage the employee to talk about the task's goals, problems he or she encountered in doing the work, and what may have gone wrong. As the person talks, give your full attention. Demonstrate that attention through body language (e.g., sitting up straight, leaning forward, maintaining eye contact), and by periodically nodding and paraphrasing what you've heard: "So, if I understand you, the sales department was not very responsive to your request for unit sales data. Is that right?" Ask questions that encourage dialogue and home in on the cause of poor performance: "Do you think that the sales department would have been more responsive if I had requested the data, not you?" You may be surprised by what you learn, and the employee will have the satisfaction of having had his or her say.

This type of positive dialogue, with each party giving and receiving feedback, will bring the two of you closer to the source of the performance problem and open the door to alternative remedies. Equally important, it will make your employee understand two things:

1. You are a results-oriented manager.
2. In accepting a delegated task, he or she accepts responsibility for specified results.

Those understandings will set the groundwork for better future performance.

Now, take a few minutes to rate yourself as a performance evaluator. Think back to conversations you have had within the past few months with employees about how well or how poorly they performed. With

FIGURE 5-1. SCORING SHEET FOR YOUR
PERFORMANCE AS AN EVALUATOR.

	Score (1–5)
I always conduct an after-action performance review with my subordinates.	
I always stick to observable facts when I evaluate someone's performance.	
I always focus on the problem, not the person.	
I always help the person understand the larger context of the performance problem.	
I always try to get the person talking about his or her problem and its possible causes.	
Total Score	
Total Score/5 = Average Score	

those situations clearly in mind, indicate how well the statements in Figure 5-1 describe you. Use a 1 to 5 scale, where 1 "least" describes you and 5 "best" describes you.

Your self-assessment in terms of each statement should get you thinking about your habits of evaluation and underscore any performance problems you have in those areas.

At this point, you've learned about each of the five steps of the delegating process. But book learning is no substitute for what you can learn from direct experience. Are you ready to put the five steps into practice? Before you do, read the next chapter, which identifies and offers practical solutions to a number of problems that delegators routinely encounter.

CHAPTER REVIEW

Try the following open-book review quiz to find out how much you've learned in this chapter:

1. How can you, as the delegator, benefit from understanding a person's performance capabilities?

_____

_____

_____

_____

_____

2. Which is more important, *what* was accomplished or *how* it was accomplished? Explain your response.

_____

_____

_____

_____

_____

3. As you evaluate the performance of a delegated task, which three areas should concern you most?

_____

_____

_____

_____

_____

4. This chapter described three psychological errors that managers often make when evaluating others. Describe one of these errors and what can be done to avoid it.

_____

_____

_____

_____

_____

5. When discussing performance problems with subordinates, why is it important to focus on the facts?

_____

_____

_____

_____

_____

CHAPTER 6

TYPICAL PROBLEMS AND HOW TO SOLVE THEM

T he previous chapters provided a five-step process you can follow
in becoming a more prolific and effective delegator. Those steps
follow a logical progression:

1. Decide what to delegate

2. Find the right person

3. Assign the task in a clear manner

4. Monitor progress and provide feedback

5. Evaluate performance

What could be more rational and straightforward? It should be simple,
right?

But as you may have discovered from experience, anything that
involves people usually falls short of being entirely rational, straightforward, and simple. It's not for nothing that Mark Twain referred to
"the cussedness of the human race." Anytime you involve people, you're
bound to have misunderstandings, differences of opinion, conflicting

expectations, diverse or incompatible work styles, and interpersonal conflict. Such are the ways of organizational life.

Delegation always involves some risk of a bad outcome, either because of failure on the employee's end, because of something the manager fails to do, or because of outside factors over which neither party has control. You must be prepared for these and for the human behaviors that occasionally throw a monkey wrench into our tidy five-step delegation process. This chapter will help you to analyze and solve the following typical delegation problems: resistance, the need to run to the boss with every problem, biting off more than can be chewed, the inability to effectively collaborate with others, the inability to take charge, miscommunication, and the inability to handle the job.

Let's now examine these problems and what you can do to solve them.

RESISTANCE

"I'd love to help with that," Oscar tells his boss, "but I'm really snowed under right now. Could someone else handle it?" That's Oscar's usual response whenever his boss, Janice, tries to delegate some special assignment to him. Janice knows that she can simply order him to take on the job. After all, she is his boss. But when tasks fall outside a person's job description and the workplace routine, Janice always tries to negotiate those extra assignments with her subordinates. "I don't like them to think that I'm piling things on them," she says.

Problem. It appears as though Oscar has Janice well trained. She'll delegate the work to someone else, or do it herself, if he simply says, "I'm snowed under." This creates an unhealthy situation. If Janice accepts work that she should delegate to Oscar, she's not managing. If she follows the path of least resistance and delegates to more willing subordinates, she will fail to maintain equity within the work group: Oscar will be skating by while his peers do all the heavy lifting, creating eventual resentment and low morale among the "worker bees" in the office. And Oscar won't gain new skills that the assignments could have given him.

Solution. Janice's first step should be to check Oscar's current workload. He claims that he doesn't have time for more tasks, but is that true? If it is true, how effectively is he currently using his time? Perhaps he would benefit from time management training. (The HR departments of many large organizations offer time management seminars for managers and employees. Does yours?) Or perhaps Oscar needs help prioritizing his work, moving some less important or time-sensitive tasks to the back burner to make room for Janice's assignment.

If Oscar is simply sandbagging to avoid additional work, Janice should exert her authority and delegate a task to him, no ifs, ands, or buts. She would be wise to begin with a small job, provide ample time, and emphasize the importance of her deadline. She should monitor Oscar's progress carefully to ensure success; he must not be allowed to deliver late or substandard work, which would help him avoid all future extra assignments. Once the first delegated task is complete, Janice should give Oscar progressively more challenging tasks.

THE NEED TO RUN TO THE BOSS
WITH EVERY PROBLEM

Unlike Oscar, Cleo is always willing to accept responsibility for a task. But her understanding of the phrase *accept responsibility* is limited—it's certainly different from what her boss understands. "She's driving me crazy," her boss says to himself. "It seems like she's in my office ten times a day with some problem: 'I'm not sure what to do about this.'; 'Where can I find that?'; 'How do you want me to handle this?' I should either delegate to someone else or do the job myself."

Problem. Cleo's willingness to accept delegated tasks is commendable, but she's clearly failing to take responsibility for the work. Occasional requests for advice and instruction are fair enough—even expected—but Cleo appears to be pushing too much of the responsibility back onto her boss's shoulders. Perhaps she is afraid she will fail at the task; perhaps she feels she does not have the authority to make certain decisions. Whatever the reason, her continual appeals for solutions and decisions are causing her boss to have to shoulder some of the responsibility and depriving Cleo of the experience of succeeding at the task.

Solution. The boss should first examine his own part in this drama. Has he given Cleo a task for which she is not prepared by experience or instruction? Has he failed to give her authority to make decisions as needed? If either or both are the case, he hasn't properly delegated the task, and it's his responsibility to provide a remedy.

If Cleo *is* properly prepared for the task, then the boss should resist her attempts to put the monkey on his back—that is, to do things and make decisions for which she took responsibility when she accepted the assignment. The next time she comes to him for a decision, he might handle it like this:

Cleo: About this assignment you asked me to do, I have to organize a meeting between people in the purchasing department and one of the inventory managers. They've been fighting over whose fault the problem is. Should I set up the meeting on the third floor, in the purchasing department, or over in Building C, where the inventory people have their offices? Or somewhere else in neutral territory?

Boss: Yes, that's an interesting problem.

Cleo: So which one do you think is best?

Boss: You're responsible for setting up the meeting, Cleo. It's your choice, not mine.

Cleo: True, but what would you do if you were me?

Boss: If I were you I'd go back to my office, think about the pros and cons of each choice, then pick the best one. Any other questions?

After a few encounters like this, Cleo will get the point and take greater responsibility for delegated tasks. Doing so will make her a better employee and further her career opportunities.

Some attempts by employees to "upwardly delegate" their work—either routine or delegated assignments—may be justified. Their schedules may be overloaded. They may lack the necessary know-how. You must decide if these attempts to push the work onto you have merit and address them—not by taking the work back, but by fixing the underlying problems that prevent the employees from succeeding at the tasks.

BITING OFF MORE THAN CAN BE CHEWED

In chapter 2, we discussed the type of person who can't say no. When you're asking for a volunteer to take on a task and everyone starts looking at his or her shoes or otherwise avoids eye contact with you, this well-meaning person will step forward. Not that she has the time to do the work (she's such a good employee that she routinely takes on more than anyone could reasonably handle). Not that she is the only person capable of doing the job. This person steps forward out of a sense of duty when no one else will. "Someone has to do it," she will tell herself.

Problem. You should cherish this type of diligent employee, especially if her capabilities match her dedication. However, you risk burning this person out if you turn too often to her. And it's an easy thing to do. A hassled manager is always tempted to approach the one person in the group who will accept yet another job without complaint. It's so easy. Unfortunately, you'll soon have this person overcommitted. Deadlines will be missed or incomplete work will be submitted.

Solution. Handle this person with care. She's valuable and, assuming that she's smart and an active learner, has tremendous promotion potential. Delegate enough work to keep her busy, but not so burdened that she'll burn out. Be sure to delegate some "fun" projects to her, not just the work that all her colleagues have rejected or avoided. Stage tasks in ways that provide progressive learning and career development.

Coach as needed to enhance her workplace skills and the learning experience. Get her into formal training programs as the situation dictates. Make sure you reward her publicly, so others will see that volunteering has benefits in the short and long term.

CONNECT YOUR BEST PEOPLE WITH MENTORS

When you have an ambitious, career-oriented subordinate with high promotion potential, connect him or her with a mentor. A mentor is a more senior and experienced person who can provide counsel and role modeling, give feedback, and open doors for a protégé who wants to learn and move up. Many organizations have formal or informal mentoring programs for promising junior employees.

Ideally, a mentor should *not* be directly above the protégé in the chain of command. While a boss can play a useful matchmaker role, being simultaneously boss and mentor is seldom a compatible combination. A boss's judgmental role is often in conflict with the mentoring role.

Which of your subordinates would benefit from having a mentor? Who would be good mentors for these individuals?

THE INABILITY TO EFFECTIVELY COLLABORATE WITH OTHERS

Carter is new to the organization but has already made a good impression on you, his manager. "This guy's a hard worker," you say, "and he does a great job with his market research duties. He's a fine individual contributor. I think I'll toss him something difficult and unusual and see how well he handles it."

Nothing about your delegated task is beyond Carter's proven technical skills. Well, almost nothing. You have asked him to design a plan for researching the market for a new product concept. "Carter, you need to get some project cost figures from the production department, talk with the ad people about the level of promotional support required, and then work with the sales department to identify three or four test market cities. I'm sure that those people will give you all the data and information you need," you tell him.

You think the job is well in hand but are surprised by what you learn at your first progress meeting with Carter. "I'm afraid that I haven't gotten very far," Carter confesses. "I have an initial research plan, but after three weeks I still haven't gotten any information or communication from the other departments. They've blown me off."

Problem. Carter needs the collaboration of others in the organization, but they aren't playing ball. What can be done?

Solution. As you investigate this problem, you should begin with yourself. You've delegated work to a strong individual contributor, but the job requires collaboration with different people and departments—none of whom owe anything to Carter. Nor does Carter have the formal or informal authority to demand their cooperation. Have you told the other departments that Carter has an important job to do and that he's acting on your behalf? Have you alerted others that you've authorized Carter to gather market information and request their collaboration? If you haven't supported Carter in these ways, you shouldn't be surprised that other departments haven't made helping him a priority and that he's running up against interdepartmental barriers.

But what if you have provided adequate support? As an individual contributor, it may be that Carter lacks the organizational skills or relationships needed to enlist interdepartmental collaboration around the research project, in which case you've delegated the task to a person ill-prepared to succeed. In this particular case, you may be able to salvage the venture by coaching, or you may need to personally intervene. If you'd like this subordinate to improve his organizational skills, working *with* him to create interdepartmental collaboration around the project could be highly beneficial.

THE INABILITY TO TAKE CHARGE

Romeo is bright and has always followed instructions well. Whenever his supervisor shows him what to do, Romeo follows through with good performance. Encouraged by the good work of her subordinate, the supervisor has delegated to him a new task: one with several parts. But this time, the results are disappointing. "I explained what I was looking for in the job and left it to him to do it his own way," the supervisor explains to a colleague. "But every time I look in on his progress, I find him stalled. He doesn't know how to move forward without specific instructions from me whenever he hits a bump in the road. He seems to want me to stand there and say, 'Do this, then do that.' It's frustrating. I'm practically doing the job myself."

Problem. This delegator has just discovered something about her subordinate that she did not understand: Romeo is not a self-starter, and maybe not a problem solver. It's not unusual to have subordinates who are effective as long as their assignments are well defined and require little or no decision-making or problem-solving skills. Many will grow out of that stage as they gain confidence and experience. However, when delegating tasks, a manager has to understand subordinate capabilities as they stand at the moment.

Solution. There are two ways the supervisor can deal with Romeo:

1. Assign him tasks but anticipate the possibility that she'll have to intervene more than she'd like with coaching, instructions, and

general hand-holding. This is the best option if one of her conscious goals is to develop Romeo's workplace capabilities.

2. Give him only well-defined tasks that require no major initiative or problem solving, or that can be broken down into discrete steps. Later, link the steps together into larger and larger assignments.

MISCOMMUNICATION

Sarah, the production manager of a small magazine publisher, has just returned from a three-week vacation. To her disappointment, she has discovered that an important project she delegated to Pete, a trusted direct report, is woefully behind schedule.

"Pete, what happened?" she asks. "Those three articles I sent you before I left for vacation should have been edited and proof-read by now, and sent to layout for the June issue."

"Gee, I'm sorry," Pete replies. "I didn't realize that they were slated for the upcoming issue."

"Well, maybe I didn't make that clear. But I did write 'Very Important' on the transmittal memo, didn't I?"

"Yeah. But you also left me two other articles, also marked 'Very Important.' I just put those two into the cue first."

Problem. A familiar communication gaffe? Probably. In communicating several projects with equal levels of importance, Sarah implicitly gave Pete discretion on how they should be prioritized in her absence. Pete did not receive the clear direction he needed to handle his boss's requests.

Solution. This example suggests three important lessons for delegators like Sarah:

1. "Very Important" assignments should always have a deadline, something that Sarah overlooked.

2. If something is really important, the delegator should communicate her intentions face-to-face, not via written memo—especially if she plans to be away on vacation for a while. A face-to-face exchange gives the subordinate a chance to ask clarifying questions and gives the delegator a chance to check for understanding. If you must use a memo, spell out your message in the most exact terms, and end the memo with "Please contact me today if you have any questions about this assignment."

3. As explained in chapter 3, the delegator should always explain the context of the assignment: how it fits in with important unit goals. In this case, Sarah should have told Pete that two of the articles had to be prepared in time for the June issue of the magazine, a key goal of the production department.

Miscommunication is the greatest enemy of effective delegation. So, be vigilant to the threat. Make your instructions and intentions crystal clear. Head off potential miscommunication by checking frequently for understanding.

THE INABILITY TO HANDLE THE JOB

During the 2007–2008 regular professional football season, the New England Patriots were undefeated. But to the disappointment of their fans, they lost their final game. That Super Bowl event proved that even champions can screw up.

If you delegate often enough, you too will screw up, even if you're a champion at assigning tasks to others. And one of the frequent causes is a failure to pick a person who can handle the job.

Problem. A person's inability to handle a job may have one or more causes: a lack of requisite skills, insufficient motivation, an already overbooked schedule. We went over this ground back in chapter 2. He or she may not have been given sufficient authority, resources, instructions, and so forth. These are potential barriers to success that the delegator should have checked for at the time the task was assigned. Uncontrollable external factors can also come into play: for example, when your subordinate is out with the flu for three days, making a shambles of her work schedule.

Solution. The way to avoid the "can't handle it" problem is to exercise great care in picking the person and assigning the task. Still, problems are bound to happen. So, how can you deal with them when they appear?

Intervention by you is needed as soon as possible. If you took the advice of chapter 4 to monitor progress at key points, you'll catch problems before they get too big to resolve. Depending on the subordinate's problem, you could:

➤ Provide more time to do the work, if feasible, by extending the deadline.

➤ Intervene with some coaching (or delegate that coaching to someone else).

➤ Take the job back and either do it yourself or hand it over to someone else. Taking the job back should be your last resort, but if quality work and timeliness are primary considerations, so be it. You win some, you lose some.

➤ If circumstances permit, allow the employee to "fail"(delivering the project late, incomplete, or imperfect), and use this as a coaching opportunity to correct the work, improve the skills, and learn from the experience. This option takes the most time, effort, and sensitivity on your part.

THE TASK IS COMPLETED . . . NOW WHAT?

Almost a week ahead of schedule, Judy has finished the task that Bob assigned to her, and, to his delight, everything is up to standards. Over the past four months, Judy spent one or two days each week on the assignment. She could do that because Bob reassigned some of her regular obligations to other employees, who took them in stride.

"Now what?" she asks Bob subsequent to the after-action review. "Now that the job is finished, how do you want me to use that time?"

Bob is momentarily perplexed. He never gave any thought about what she'd do once the job was finished, but Judy obviously can't be expected to sit around doing nothing one or two days each week. So he does what every experienced manager does when cornered: He plays for time. "Great question, Judy. I was thinking about that only yesterday. Let's talk about that tomorrow afternoon."

Problem. A long-term delegated assignment becomes part of a person's work routine, and the completion of the assignment creates a void that must be filled. The most obvious solution would be to give back to Judy all the tasks that Bob had off-loaded to other people in the department, creating small workload rebalancing needs along the way. But this might not be the best thing to do. First, if everyone else is successfully carrying his own load plus a small portion of Judy's, why disrupt the status quo? Are those other people complaining about being overworked? Have they adjusted their own capacities to absorb the added work? Did they agree to take on the work Bob delegated to them only temporarily, or has it become part of their routine?

Second, Judy may not be the same employee she was four months ago, when she first accepted the assignment. If that assignment forced her to take on greater responsibility, to learn new skills, and to build new working relationships within the company, then she's no longer the same employee. Asking Judy to return to what she was doing earlier might be, for her, a motivation-killing step backward.

Solution. The problem in Judy's case is one with which every manager must periodically wrestle: balancing or optimizing individual workloads in ways that make the most of people's capabilities and that result in the company or unit accomplishing its goals. Every case has one or more solutions based on the facts of the situation. In Judy's case, the solution might be to find yet another skill-expanding chore for her to do, perhaps one that her boss had been doing himself.

CHAPTER REVIEW

Try the following open-book review quiz to find out how much you've learned in this chapter:

1. How would you deal with a subordinate who routinely resists delegation?

_____

_____

_____

_____

_____

2. Explain one approach to dealing with a person who runs to you whenever he or she encounters a problem.

_____

_____

_____

_____

3. What's the danger in delegating to a person who chronically takes on more work than he or she can handle?

_____

_____

_____

_____

4. This chapter offered two solutions for an employee who is unable to take charge of delegated tasks and needs to be told what to do at every turn. Describe one.

_____

_____

_____

_____

_____

5. If miscommunication is the greatest enemy of effective delegation, what can you do to reduce the chance of its occurrence?

_____

_____

_____

_____

_____

CHAPTER 7

FIVE-DAY SHAPE-UP PLAN

ikc most of the things that managers and supervisors do, delegating skill can be developed through repeated practice. Think back to your first experience with coaching a subordinate, giving feedback, or disciplining a slacker. You probably said something like this when it was over: "I sure messed that up." On the other hand, you probably now recognize how much better you have become through experience. The same is true of delegating. If you look for opportunities to delegate tasks, do it often, and make a conscious effort to understand your own performance, you will become better at it.

In this final chapter, we challenge you to take a five-day shape-up plan that will put you in a practice mode. We've even provided a checklist and a worksheet that you can use to better follow the steps of the delegating process described in previous chapters.

THINKING AHEAD

Here's how the shape-up plan works. For each of five days, use the checklist in Figure 7-1 (or create one of your own) to prompt you to:

> Identify an assignable task.

> Identify an appropriate person to take on that task.

> Note the key points you should discuss when assigning the task.

> Agree on a checkpoint at which you will monitor the person's progress and provide feedback, coaching, or whatever else is needed to ensure success.

> Set a deadline for completion.

If you delegate at least one job each day for five days, you will get into the habit of consciously looking for opportunities and following through. And if you fill in each column of the checklist as you move along, you won't simply be "winging" it; instead, you will be approaching the process in a disciplined manner. This is important; if you aim to establish a habit, you don't want it to be a flawed habit.

AFTER-ACTION EVALUATION

Delegating a task is, of course, only half the job. You must follow up with an evaluation of the person's performance—both for your benefit and for his or her benefit. The worksheet in Figure 7-2 will help you approach the evaluation phase in a disciplined and systematic way. Using a scale of 1 to 5 (with 5 being excellent), rate the person's performance in the three dimensions we covered in chapter 5: completeness, timeliness, and quality. Add comments as appropriate to jog your memory when you revisit this evaluation sheet. The actual number ratings need not be shared with the person; you can make your appraisal through verbal feedback. However, making and keeping a written record will help you remember how things turned out and provide a baseline for assessing that person's progress over time.

The worksheet also asks you to think about and record:

> The person's observed strengths and weaknesses

> Areas in which future training or coaching may be needed

> Types of assignments this individual is capable of performing in the future

FIGURE 7-1. DELEGATION CHECKLIST.

	Day 1	Day 2	Day 3	Day 4	Day 5
Task to be assigned					
Candidate for the job					
Points to discuss when making the assignment					
When I will check progress					
Task deadline					

FIGURE 7-2. WORKSHEET FOR
AFTER-ACTION EVALUATION.

Date:		
Name:		
Delegated task:		

Evaluation		
		Comments
How complete?	1–5: ____	
Timeliness?	1–5: ____	
Job Quality?	1–5: ____	
Observed strengths and weaknesses		
Future training or coaching needed		
Types of future assignments this person is prepared to take on		
Self-Evaluation		
What did I do well?		
What could I have done better?		

Managers and supervisors should understand their people as well as possible in many different dimensions. This exercise will help you do that.

WHAT ABOUT YOU?

Self-evaluation is the final part of our five-day drill. Objective, after-action self-evaluation—for delegation and for everything else we do—is the key to improvement. Regrettably, this is something that many of us often fail to consider. Being busy or otherwise preoccupied, we don't always reflect back on recent experiences and capture their lessons. That's unfortunate because it retards personal growth and improvement.

What part of the delegation process did you do well? What could you have done better? Did you define and communicate the desired outcomes? Did you set up a mutually agreeable deadline and establish appropriate check-in points along the way? Were your quality, cost, and schedule requirements clear? Did you provide appropriate resources and authority to the employee? Ponder these questions and enter your observations on the worksheet in Figure 7-2. If you handled something badly (e.g., "I forgot to explain to Sally *why* the task was important when I assigned the job to her"), mentally replay that part, but this time do it right. This simple exercise when undertaken in the right spirit may prevent you from making the same mistake again in the future.

You may be thinking, "I don't need a silly self-evaluation worksheet to learn from experience." Perhaps you don't. Most of us conduct some type of unconscious self-assessment as we do our work, and these self-assessments register in our psyches. However, we can squeeze more learning from our experiences if our reflections are deliberate and methodical, as recommended here. If something didn't work according to plan, don't simply tell yourself, "Well, I'll be more careful in the future." Instead, consciously ask these questions of yourself:

"Why didn't it work well?"

"What was the root cause of the problem?"

"Were alternative approaches available?"

"If alternatives were available, why didn't I consider them?"

"Which alternative course of action, in hindsight, would have been the best choice?"

Try this self-conscious approach to your delegating experiences over the course of the five-day shape-up plan and watch your results improve.

CHAPTER REVIEW

Try the following open-book review quiz to find out how much you've learned in this chapter:

1. Describe one management or supervisory function that you've been able to master through repeated practice. How many times did you have to practice that function before you could observe tangible and significant improvement?

_____

_____

_____

_____

_____

2. How often do you pause to consciously review and learn from your experiences as a manager or supervisor?

_____

_____

_____

_____

_____

3. The checklist shown in Figure 7-2 asks you to record your thoughts on three aspects of your subordinate's performance with a delegated task. One was "Observed strengths and weaknesses." Can you name the other two and comment on why those evaluations are useful to you as a manager?

_____

_____

_____

_____

_____

AFTERWORD

D elegating may seem like a small activity in the broad universe of things that managers do every day. Yet its effective use draws on and develops many other skills that every manager must have: accomplishing work through others, giving feedback, coaching, conducting performance evaluations, and so forth. So, when you're delegating, you're exercising lots of different management muscles.

This WorkSmart book has given you a five-step process and a five-day plan to get your delegating skills on the road to continuous improvement. Good luck!

GLOSSARY

Checkpoint
A predetermined point at which progress will be observed and evaluated.

Coaching
A method used by managers and supervisors to overcome performance problems and to develop the skills of their subordinates. Coaching can be provided informally and on the spot or through scheduled sessions.

360-degree feedback
An appraisal method in which anonymous information about an individual's workplace performance is collected from people who regularly interact with that person: subordinates, work team members, and internal customers.

Employee empowerment
A workplace philosophy that gives subordinates substantial discretion in how they accomplish their objectives.

Feedback
A communication process by which output (information) is returned, or "fed back," to its source as a means of regulating the situation.

Halo effect
An unconscious cognitive bias that allows a manager's judgment of a person in one category to carry over to another, unrelated category.

Isolated incident bias
A tendency of managers to allow a person's poor performance in one instance to shape their entire perception of that person.

Performance review
A practice, usually done annually, used to appraise employee performance, identify areas in need of training or coaching, and communicate employee goals for the coming year. These reviews, based on face-to-face meetings between managers and their direct reports, are also used to make decisions about bonuses and promotions.

Personal difference bias
A natural tendency to be more accepting of individuals who resemble oneself—by race, religion, educational background, political beliefs, gender, and so forth—and to be less accepting of people perceived as "different."

Quality
In the context of delegating, a job done right and on time.

SELECTED READINGS

There are many books on delegating, but, because of the near absence of the academic literature on the subject, they are short and, like this one, based largely on the workplace experiences of their authors. If you wish to learn more, we suggest that you explore publications that investigate broader skills of management that relate closely to delegating. These include the following:

Cohen, Allan R. *The Portable MBA in Management.* New York: John Wiley & Sons, 1993.

Higgins, Jaime, and Diana Smith. "Four Myths of Feedback," *Harvard Business Review,* June–July 1999.

Luecke, Richard. *Harvard Business Essentials: Coaching and Mentoring.* Boston: Harvard Business School Publishing, 2004.

———. *Harvard Business Essentials: Performance Management.* Boston: Harvard Business School Publishing, 2006.

McIntosh, Perry, and Richard Luecke. *Becoming a Manager.* New York: American Management Association, 2009.

INDEX

ability, proven vs. potential, 24
accountability, 2
action plan, 38
annual performance reviews, 60
assembly-line job, 37
authority, 2, 40–41
   ambiguity and, 39
   sharing, 5

bias, in performance evaluation, 65–66
"big picture" explanation, in task assignment, 34–36
body language, 68
boss, tasks delegated to you by, 16
burnout, risk of, 77

capability of subordinate, 24–25
challenge, as motivation, 36
changes in assignment, and performance evaluation, 62
checklists and worksheets
   delegation checklist, 89
   performance evaluation, 69, 90

subordinate identification for task, 29
   task assignment checklist, 45
checkpoints, 44–45, 50–51, 52, 95
coaching, 55–57
   avoiding common mistakes, 57
   defined, 95
   after failure, 83
   hands-on, 24–25
   level required, 13–14
collaboration, ineffective, 78–80
command-and-control management, 27
communicating evaluation to employee, 66–69
   addressing shortcomings, 67–69
   including specifics, 66–67
communication
   problems from errors in, 81–82
   written vs. face-to-face meeting, 82
complex assignments, formal schedules for, 43–44
"constructive criticism," 52
cooperation, 79
coordination problems, avoiding, 12

deadline, 81
  and evaluating performance, 62
  gaining agreement on, 43-45
  and task delegation, 14
decision-making power, 40-41
delegation
  checklist, 89
  of coaching, 56
  defined, 2
  failure, vii
  importance, 3
  indicators of wrong levels, 2
  practicing, 87
  risk of bad outcome, 74
  steps to successful, 6
  to team, 12
  see also problems in delegating; tasks
    eligible for delegation
deliverables, gaining agreement on, 43-45
description, in feedback, 53
details, providing in task assignment,
    37-41
dialogue, in sharing performance evalua-
    tion, 68
"dirty work" category of tasks, balancing
    delegation, 17
disciplinary actions, 15-16

employees
  development, 5
  empowerment, 26-27, 95
  who can't say no, 22, 77-78
  see also subordinates
empowerment, 95
  as motivator, 37
evaluating performance, 15, 59-71,
    88-90, 96
  annual, 60
  benefits, 60
  communication to employee, 66-67
  completeness, 61-62
  focus on results, 61-64
  other criteria, 64
  potential pitfalls, 65-66
  quality standards, 63-64
  scoring sheet, 69

self-assessment, 68-69
  timelines, 62
  worksheet, 90
expectations, evaluating success in
    reaching, 61
"experience curve," 63

face-to-face meeting, vs. written commu-
    nication, 82
facts, supporting negative evaluation
    comments with, 67
feedback, 49, 52-55, 96
  checkpoints for, 52
  on employee performance, 60
  rating, 55
filling void after completed assignment,
    83-85
firing, 15-16
Fletcher, Frank, 38-39
formal training, 25

Gantt chart, 43-44
goals, linking to task, 35

halo effect, 65, 96
Halsey, William, 38-39
"hand-off errors," avoiding, 12
Harvard Business Review, 57
hesitation to delegate, 3-5
hiring process, 14-15
human capital, companies valuing, 27

interdepartmental collaboration, 79
interest in task, generating, 23
isolated incident bias, 65, 96

judgmental attitude, and feedback, 53

listening
  in coaching, 57
  in feedback, 54

management
  classic functions, 1-2
  shared and unique skills, 11-13
  workload levels, 1

means, vs. outcomes, 41
    as evaluation focus, 61–64
measurable quality, 63
mentors, 78
micromanagement, 5, 51
miscommunication, 81–82
modifiable behavior, feedback on, 53
monitoring progress, 49–58
    without micromanaging, 51
monkey, refusal to take back, 57–58,
    76–77
motivation, in task assignment, 36–37

Nucor Corporation, 16

off-site subordinates, monitoring,
    51–52
Oncken, William, Jr., 57
opportunity cost, 4
outcomes, vs. means, 41
    as evaluation focus, 61–64
overcommitted employees, 77–78
overdelegation, 2
ownership of assignment, 37

path of least resistance, 74
performance evaluation, 15, 59–71,
    88–90, 96
    annual, 60
    benefits, 60
    communication to employee,
        66–67
    completeness, 61–62
    focus on results, 61–64
    other criteria, 64
    potential pitfalls, 65–66
    quality standards, 63–64
    scoring sheet, 69
    self-assessment, 68–69
    timelines, 62
    worksheet, 90
performance standards, for subordinates,
    5
personal attacks, avoiding in negative
    evaluation, 67
personal difference bias, 65–66, 96

praise, specifics in, 66–67
priorities
    clarifying, 81
    help with setting, 75
    and task scheduling, 21
problem solving, delegating to those
    closest, 26
problems, vs. person, in negative evalua-
    tion, 67
problems in delegating, 73–86
    filling void after completed
        assignment, 83–85
    inability to handle job, 82–83
    inability to take charge, 80–81
    ineffective collaboration, 78–80
    miscommunication, 81–82
    person who can't say no, 22, 77–78
    resistance, 74–75
    running to boss with every problem,
        75–77
promotion, loss of opportunity, 5–6

quality of work, 13–14, 96
    in performance evaluation, 63–64
    setting example, 63
questions, from subordinates, 42–43

recognition, as motivator, 36
recurring tasks, delegation, 13
reliability, for task, 24–25
remote locations, monitoring work at,
    51–52
resistance, 74–75
resource support discussion, 39–40
responsibility, 2, 4–5
    employee acceptance, 75
    inability to take charge, 80–81
    as motivation, 36
    start-to-finish, 37

schedules, for complex assignments,
    43–44
self-assessment
    of delegation skills, 90–91
    of performance evaluation, 68–69
self-improvement, interest in, 56

shape-up plan, 87–92
    after-action evaluation, 88–90
    delegation checklist, 89
    self-assessment, 90–91
    thinking ahead, 87–88
skills, shared and unique, between man-
    agers and subordinates, 11–13
Southwest Airlines, 14
specificity of feedback, 54
Spruance, Ray, 38–39
start-to-finish responsibility, 37
subordinate identification for task,
    19–31
    capability and reliability, 24–25
    closeness to problem, 26–27
    interest in task, 22–23
    potential to benefit from assignment,
        27–28
    questions to ask, 28
    spreading work around, 25
    time available, 21–22
    worksheet, 29
subordinates
    communicating evaluation to, 66–67
    developing competencies of, 3
    discretion in meeting objectives,
        26–27
    empowering, 26–27, 95
    failure, 50
    failure to develop, 5–6
    monitoring off-site, 51–52
    opportunity for response to
        evaluation, 68
    overcommitted, 77–78
    performance standards for, 5
    planning time after task completion,
        83–85
    questions from, 42–43
    shared and unique skills, 11–13
    who can't say no, 22, 77–78

task
    delegated to you by boss, 16
    eliminating unnecessary, 35
    inability to handle, 82–83
task assignment, 33–47

agreement on deliverables and dead-
    lines, 43–45
authority and decision-making power,
    40–41
"big picture" explanation in, 34–36
checklist, 45
giving details, 37–41
motivation in, 36–37
questions from subordinates, 42–43
resource support discussion, 39–40
specifics on expected outcome, 41
tasks eligible for delegation, 9–18
    "dirty work" category, 17
    individual responsibility for, 12
    quality of work, 13–14
    shared and unique skills, 11–13
    subordinate interest in, 22–23
tasks never delegated, 14–16
team, delegation to, 12
360-degree feedback, 15, 95
time requirements
    for delegated task, 4
    estimating, 62–63
    of feedback, 54
    and subordinate identification for
        task, 21–22
    for training, 13
training, time requirements, 13
tribalism, 66
trust, 39
    and delegation, 3–4

underdelegation, 2
unique skills, between managers and
    subordinates, 11–13
upward delegation of work, 76–77

void, filling after completed assignment,
    83–85

Wass, Donald L., 57
"whole" jobs, delegating, 37
work, refusal to accept incomplete,
    62
work-at-home employees, monitoring,
    51–52

Announcing!

workload levels, optimizing, 84–85
workplace culture, 26–27
worksheets and checklists
    delegation checklist, 89
    performance evaluation, 69, 90

subordinate identification for task, 29
task assignment checklist, 45
World War II, Battle of Midway, 38–39
written communication, vs. face-to-face
    meeting, 82